CROSS ROADS

Old Testament

Author
Richard J. Reichert

BROWN-ROA
A Division of Harcourt Brace & Company

BROWN-ROA
A Division of Harcourt Brace & Company

Our Mission

The primary mission of BROWN-ROA is to provide the Catholic and Christian educational markets with the highest quality catechetical print and media resources. The content of these resources reflects the best insights of current theology, methodology, and pedagogical research. The resources are practical and easy to use, designed to meet expressed market needs, and written to reflect the teachings of the Catholic Church.

Nihil Obstat
Rev. Richard L. Schaefer
Imprimatur
✠ Most Rev. Jerome Hanus, O.S.B.
Archbishop of Dubuque
January 4, 1998
Feast of Saint Elizabeth Ann Seton

The Imprimatur is an official declaration that a book or pamphlet is free of doctrinal or moral error. No implication is contained therein that anyone who granted the Imprimatur agrees with the contents, opinions, or statements expressed.

Copyright © 1999 by BROWN-ROA, a division of Harcourt Brace and Company

All rights reserved. No part of this publication may be reproduced or transmitted in any form or by any means, electronic or mechanical, including photocopy, recording, or any information storage and retrieval system, without permission in writing from the publisher.

Requests for permission to make copies of any part of the work should be mailed to the following address: Permissions Department, Harcourt Brace & Company, 6277 Sea Harbor Drive, Orlando, Florida 32887-67777.

Portions of this work were published in previous editions.
Excerpts from the English translation of the *Catechism of the Catholic Church* for use in the United States of America Copyright © 1994, United States Catholic Conference, Inc.—Libreria Editrice Vaticana. Used with Permission.

The Scripture quotations contained herein are from the New Revised Standard Version Bible: Catholic Edition copyright © 1993 and 1989 by the Division of Christian Education of the National Council of the Churches of Christ in the U.S.A. Used by permission. All rights reserved.

Illustrations: Rob Suggs

Photo Credits: Nancy Anne Dawe—18, 77; Editorial Development Associates—2, 31, 50, 56–57; Mimi Forsyth—29, 41, 81; Gene Plaisted, OSC/CROSIERS—6, 63, 90, 99, 105; Robert Roethig—24, 69; James L. Shaffer—7, 34, 44, 46, 54, 58, 67, 73, 88, 91, 98; Skjold Photography—9, 13, 22, 84

Printed in the United States of America

ISBN 0-15-950468-6

10 9 8 7 6 5 4 3 2 1

Unburying the Treasure

Introduction

Dear Adventurer

To officially be called an "adventurer," one who seeks a challenging experience, you must be willing to take on the challenge of discovery. As a young person, you are probably someone who wants to take on the challenge of discovering life and all that it holds. One of the greatest discoveries for all of us is the uncovering of the mysteries of the Bible, the greatest treasure to ever be found. To accomplish this goal, you must be willing to take on the challenge of acquainting yourself with the Old Testament.

THE TREASURE HUNT BEGINS

How many of these nuggets of treasure have you already discovered?

1. What Old Testament person is called the "father of faith"?
2. The first king of Israel was David. True or False?
3. What kind of trick did Jacob play on his father?
4. What unit of measurement was used to build the ark?
5. What was the name of the miraculous food God fed the Israelites in the desert?
6. Who was promised that a messiah would be chosen from his family?
7. Isaiah was (a) a king of Israel, (b) a prophet, (c) an Egyptian pharaoh.
8. Which Israelite king was famous for his wisdom?
9. Sarah was the wife of which famous Israelite leader?
10. The most important Israelite feast was (a) Passover, (b) Hanukkah, (c) Pentecost.

Don't feel bad if you didn't know many of the answers. It just means you have lots of treasure to search for. The following are clues to aid you in your search:

1. *Introduction to the Greatest Book Ever Discovered*
   - Digging tools
   - Deciphering codes
   - Organizing new discoveries
2. *You Shall Be Called Abraham*
   - Uncovering God and God's plan
   - Committing to be the people of God
3. *Passover, Exodus, and Covenant*
   - Exiting excitement—the Passover
   - Journeying with hope and despair—the Exodus
   - Giving promises, breaking promises—the covenant
4. *From Judges to Kings*
   - Testing by the Israelites
   - Testing by God
5. *A Short-Lived Golden Age*
   - Abounding wealth and power
   - Ensuing greed and abuse
6. *Prophets, Kings, and Conquerors*
   - Continuing the testing
   - Proceeding with modernization and war
7. *A Nation Rebuilds*
   - Returning to exile
   - Living in hope
8. *End of an Era*
   - Living with the Romans
   - Awaiting the messiah

By taking on the adventure of uncovering the Old Testament, you are accepting the challenge of uncovering the mysteries of our faith to better understand what it means to us today. This challenge is only for those who are willing to try to learn more about their faith through the stories of the Old Testament. Let's grab our shovels and start digging for that treasure!

1

Introduction to the Greatest Book Ever Discovered

". . . For the LORD will again take delight in prospering you, just as he delighted in prospering your ancestors, when you obey the LORD your God by observing his commandments and decrees that are written in this book of the law, because you turn to the LORD your God with all your heart and with all your soul." (Deuteronomy 30:9b–10)

"Flick Your BIQ" (Bible IQ)

Instructions: See how much you already know about the Bible. Circle the words that you would find in the Bible.

apple
ark
banana
boat
cathedral
Catholic
Christmas
David
fortune teller
Hanukkah
Hebrew
Henry
Israelites
Jesus
king
manna
Passover
patriarchs
pharaoh
pilgrims
president
prophet
sacrifice
temple

Discovering the treasure

In 1981, Steven Spielberg excited audiences with the adventures of an archaeologist who uncovered the ark of the covenant in the movie, "Raiders of the Lost Ark." Viewers wanted to be like Indiana Jones, finding the lost ark and actually proving a piece of our biblical history. Despite the stunts and the battles with the enemy, it was Indiana Jones' respect and understanding of the sacredness of the ark that brought him success. It is our hope that with this course, you, too, will gain an understanding of the sacredness of the Bible that will bring you success as well.

CATECHISM CLIP

Through all the words of Sacred Scripture, God speaks only one single Word, his one Utterance in whom he expresses himself completely. [Cf. Heb *1:1–3.] (102)*

Should you accept this adventure?

Every couple of years, it seems, there is a report of some miraculous appearance of the Blessed Virgin or Jesus. If the report sounds believable, thousands of people from all over the world travel to that spot hoping to receive some **revelation** from God. If you really believed that you could get some direct revelation from God by going to such a place, would you go? Now be honest. Chances are, you would.

Revelation—to make something that was a secret or hidden, publicly or generally known

Mary Sighting

Can you name one place where a miraculous appearance has been reported? Who appeared to whom? What do you believe about this appearance?

Archaeological excavations near Bethlehem

The fact is, you don't have to travel halfway around the world to experience direct revelation from God. At this minute, somewhere in your own house is a Bible that can provide you with God's revelation. Also, God can appear to you indirectly in very ordinary, human experiences such as within the words of your friend, or through a sunset, or within a great victory on the playing field.

God Sighting!

If God the Father, Mary, or Jesus chose to appear to you, describe how and where you believe this miraculous appearance would happen.

You may feel the Bible is difficult to read. That's normal enough. But the answer to the question "Why should you accept this adventure of getting to know the Bible?" is simple. The Bible reveals God to you! It reveals all that God wants to tell you about who God really is, who you really are, and what is really important in life. Uncovering the Bible helps you uncover your faith—where it came from, where it is today with all its questions and concerns, and where it may take you in the future.

Is the treasure worth seeking?

As in all adventures we take on, this one may not be easy. That's why we like adventures! If you are willing to make the effort now to learn a few basic facts about what's in the Bible, how it is put together, and how to approach it, the Bible will become a treasure for you. It will provide you with hands-on contact with God's direct revelation for the rest of your life.

Tools for the adventure

To begin, you must learn your way around the site you are exploring. The Bible consists of two sections known as the Old Testament and the New Testament. The Old Testament includes the Hebrew Scriptures.The New Testament is sometimes called the Christian Scriptures. You must learn how to **decipher** "the code" that will help you learn how to find books in each of these sections. A passage from the Bible is cited like this: Gen. 13:1–12. *Gen.* is the abbreviation for *Genesis,* and refers to the book in the Bible where the passage is located. The number *13* refers to the thirteenth chapter in the Book of Genesis. The numbers *1–12* refer to verses one through twelve in the thirteenth chapter.

Decipher—to interpret, explain, or make clear

Gen. 13:1–12

The Book of Genesis, the chapter, the verses

Skim through your Bible to find the list of abbreviations for each of the books in the Old Testament of your Bible.

Get to Work! Part 1

Using this information, see if you can find the following Scripture passages, and write the first three words and the last three words in each passage.

- Genesis 13:1–9
- Exodus 17:1–7
- Job 7:1–6
- Psalm 108:1–7
- Isaiah 44:9–12

Some writers needed more than one book to relate their stories or information to their audiences. When this happens you will find the code contains an additional number in front of the book's title. Samuel is an example of such a writer. Passages from his books would be cited like this: 1 Samuel 2:1–10 and 2 Samuel 18:9–18.

Get to Work! Part 2

Find the Contents page in your Bible. List the names of authors who wrote more than one book in the Hebrew Scriptures.

____

____

____

Scripture Search

Read 1 Kings 19:1–13.
What does this passage say about who or what God is?

____

____

____

How do you expect to hear God?

____

____

____

The tools of organization—the books of the Hebrew Scriptures

There are various ways to group the books of the Hebrew Scriptures. The following is one of the more common divisions used by scholars.

The Books of the Law—The Pentateuch

Genesis
Exodus
Leviticus
Numbers
Deuteronomy

The Historical Books

Joshua
Judges
Ruth
1 and 2 Samuel
1 and 2 Kings
1 and 2 Chronicles
Ezra
Nehemiah

The Prophets

Major Prophets	*Minor Prophets*	
Isaiah	Joel	Nahum
Jeremiah	Amos	Habakkuk
Lamentations	Obadiah	Zephaniah
Ezekiel	Hosea	Haggai
Daniel	Jonah	Zechariah
	Micah	Malachi

The Wisdom Books—The Writings

Wisdom	Song of Songs
Psalms	Ecclesiastes
Proverbs	Job

These books (or parts of them) are included in the Catholic and Orthodox Christian Old Testament.

Tobit	1 and 2 Maccabees
Judith	Baruch
Esther	Sirach

Get to Work! Part 3

To see how the Bible you are using organizes the books of the Hebrew Scriptures, check its table of contents. Count how many books there are for each of the following categories:

The Books of the Law ______
The Historical Books ______
The Prophets ______

The Major Prophets ______
The Minor Prophets ______
The Wisdom Books ______

Oldest first!

The first part of the Bible, called the Old Testament and including the Hebrew Scriptures, is what we're going to be studying in this course. This is the oldest and richest part of the Bible and the part that can be the hardest to understand.

Let's begin with this quick outline of the key historical periods and events of the Hebrew people that are covered in the Hebrew Scriptures.

Historical Outline

?	1750	1500	1200	1020	922	722	586	536	Birth of Jesus
B.C.E.									† C.E.

Pre-History *From ??? to about 1750 B.C.E.*

The pre-history is contained in the first twelve chapters of the first book of the Bible—Genesis. These chapters tell some of the most famous Bible stories, such as the stories of creation, Adam and Eve, Cain and Abel, Noah and the flood, and the Tower of Babel.

Age of the Patriarchs *1750–1500 B.C.E.*

This is the period of the beginning of the Hebrew people through Abraham and Sarah. It is the time of Isaac and Rebekah, Jacob and Esau and their wives, Jacob's twelve sons, and especially his son, Joseph.

Slavery in Egypt: the Exodus *1500–1200 B.C.E.*

This is the central event in the history of the Hebrew people. Abraham's descendants fall into slavery in Egypt. It is the time of Moses, the plagues and the Passover, the Exodus or escape through the Red Sea, the giving of the covenant, and the stories of the Hebrews in the desert.

Period of the Judges *1200–1020 B.C.E.*

During this time, the Hebrews struggle to form a respectable kingdom and settle in the promised land.

The Kingdom Established *1020–922 B.C.E.*

This is the period of Kings Saul, David, and Solomon. It is a high point in terms of worldly power in the history of the Hebrew people. The Temple is built during this time.

Civil War and Divided Kingdom *922–722 B.C.E.*

Because of civil war, the kingdom David established is split into the northern and southern kingdoms. The northern kingdom gradually drifts farther and farther from the covenant and is eventually conquered by foreign powers. It completely disappears by 722 B.C.E.

The Southern Kingdom *722–586 B.C.E*

The southern kingdom lasts another one hundred and fifty years but it, too, is eventually conquered. The Temple is destroyed and many of the surviving Hebrew people are carried off to Babylon.

Exile *586–536 B.C.E.*

This fifty-year period is a low point for God's people. They have no Temple, no land, and no apparent hope for the future.

Post-Exile *536 B.C.E.–Birth of Jesus*

During this period, the Hebrews return to the promised land. They rebuild the Temple and attempt to reestablish themselves as a kingdom, but they are often at war and are conquered by various foreign powers, the last of whom are the Romans. Finally, the promised Messiah, Jesus, is born.

Check It Out! ☑

All Bibles had to be copied by hand until 1450 C.E. when the printing press was invented. Hand-copied Bibles were so rare and expensive in the Middle Ages that a Bible displayed in a church was often chained to its stand so thieves wouldn't steal it.

Why is this a mystery, a puzzle?

If the main story of the Old Testament is an easily outlined story, you'd think reading the Bible would be simple. But, as you probably already know, the Bible seems like a puzzle. It's a puzzle for two reasons. First, the Bible isn't one book with many chapters. It's more like a library or collection of many different books, written by different authors at different times using different styles of writing. Second, many of the individual books in the Bible were edited and reworked by different authors at various other times. Even the individual books can be a mixture of historical facts, poetry, and politics. One thing is important as you begin to read the Bible, **don't try to read the Bible the way you read other books!**

Timeline—Small-group activity

Draw a timeline of events for your class by breaking your class's life span into two- to four-year periods. In small groups, choose one of the sections of the timeline and together write an essay, poem, or newspaper article about the events that happened during that time. Combine all the written efforts of your classmates into one book. What do you notice about this book? How are the style and the way that your book was written similar to that of the Bible?

Written in stages

The Hebrew Scriptures, and in fact the whole Old Testament, were put together in stages over many centuries.

Stage One: The Oral Tradition

Instead of writing down details of events, the people would pass the information on by word of mouth. Events of the time became the stories and the gossip shared from family to family and tribe to tribe.

Take, for example, the story of the Exodus. Those who lived through the event would tell their children what happened, or what Moses said, or what it was like in the desert. These stories would then be kept alive, passed down from one generation to another. In the process, of course, different versions of the same key event developed from one campfire to the next. Remember, these people told stories around the campfires in the evening as a form of entertainment, so their recall of events was very good. Different people remembered various parts as important, so the stories changed a bit with each retelling during this **oral tradition stage.**

Oral tradition stage—stories remembered by *telling* others about the event

Telephone!—Small-group activity

Get into a group of six. One person begins the game by whispering a message into the ear of the person to their right. The message is then passed on to the next person and so on until it reaches the final person. The last person to receive the message must repeat it aloud to see if the message was passed correctly. Try to make things more difficult with a longer message or a tongue twister. Discuss in your group how good you were at repeating oral tradition.

"Telephone" in Action

Can you identify one story that is continually repeated in your family, year after year? (Examples may be how your parents first met, a favorite or strange holiday happening or tradition, a funny story of what you used to act like as a child, etc.) What do you notice happening to this story as it is told and retold?

Stage Two: The Written Tradition

Eventually, some people took it upon themselves to write down one of these versions of the story. People began to collect these different written accounts. Thus, the Bible moved to the **written collection stage.**

Written collection stage—stories remembered through various written versions of the same event

Reporter of the News—Small-group activity

Have everyone try to write a description of a common event that all members of the group took part in. Examples may be a recent trip the group was on or an event the group attended. Have each person read their accounts of the event and discuss how similar or dissimilar the events are when they are put into written form.

Stage Three: The Synthesis Stage

In many cases, just a few centuries before Jesus, other writers began to attempt to put all these various collections together. These editors used a "pick and choose" approach. In some cases, when they had two accounts of the same event, or two versions of some prophet's teaching, they would choose one and not include the other. In other cases, they decided to include both accounts, for both had some important details they wanted to save. That's why we sometimes have two or even three different versions of the same event in the Bible.

Scripture Search

Read the two different accounts of creation found in Genesis (Genesis 1:1–2:4a [version one] and Genesis 2:4b–23 [version two]) and identify two similarities and two differences between the stories.

Similarities

____

____

Differences

____

____

Editors of the Bible tried to group the various writings together according to types of writings or who the authors were. Because of this, the events are often not listed in the order they may have happened. For example, all the psalms were grouped together based on their poetic style. The prophetic books are listed together because the authors were all known as prophets. A category of books may have been written by many different people who may have lived hundreds of years apart.

Check It Out

The *canon*, or official list of the Hebrew Scriptures, was not established until 90 C.E. by rabbis and scribes who escaped the destruction of Jerusalem in 70 C.E.

Check It Out

The original Hebrew Scriptures were, of course, written in Hebrew. The Hebrew alphabet is different from ours because it has twenty-two letters and no vowels and is written and read from right to left.

Written with hindsight

Suppose you discovered your family had to move to another part of the country next week. As you go through the actual move, you may feel frightened and angry or perhaps excited and happy. A few weeks after the move you write a friend and tell him or her how you feel. Now suppose it's one year later. You look back on that move and may have an entirely different feeling about it. What seemed terrible at the time may now seem like the best thing that ever happened to you, the turning point in your life. Or what first seemed good, you now realize, was the worst thing that could have happened. So if you wrote your friend a year later, the second letter could be quite different from the first. The point is, having experienced the event, your feelings may be totally different than what they were before or during the event. This type of "after the fact" knowledge is called **hindsight.**

Hindsight—knowledge gained from looking back at an experience or event

The Bible was written by using hindsight of past events. In the case of the Bible, the people kept reviewing the old events in light of the new experiences they had. Therefore, they would gain new insights into the real meaning of the old events and add these reflections to the writings.

So what you have in the finished version of the Hebrew Scriptures is the collected wisdom the people gained throughout those centuries, inspired by the Holy Spirit and edited into remembered stories.

After the Fact

You were probably disappointed when you found out the real identity of Santa Claus and the Easter Bunny. Using hindsight, what understanding do you now have of why parents pretend that they exist?

CATECHISM CLIP

*In Sacred Scripture, the Church constantly finds her nourishment and her strength, for she welcomes it not as a human word, "but as what it really is, the word of God." [*1 Thess *2:13; cf* DV *24.] In the sacred books, the Father who is in heaven comes lovingly to meet his children, and talks with them. [* DV *21.] (104)*

Myths and legends

Yes, there is a Santa Claus. Maybe!

Describe the scene when you first learned that Santa Claus was not a real person. Be sure to include your reaction and your feelings. How do you feel about Santa Claus today? How do you pass on the legend of this person to those who still believe?

Many of the stories of our lives revolve around characters that are not necessarily historical, but could represent how we act. For example, in the mythical story of the Tortoise and the Hare, we realistically know that these two animals did not really race. What we do know is that they symbolize types of people and that despite outward appearances, people can "win" even when the odds seem against them. These types of symbolic stories are called myths or legends.

Myth—a fictitious story that tries to explain a custom, tradition, or a reason why things happen as they do
Legend—a possibly true story handed down from the past

The Bible contains a number of these myths and legends. Though both of these are stories based on truth, there is a significant difference between them. A myth gives us a deep, universal truth using a "made-up" story with symbols everyone can understand. A legend generally begins as a real event in history, but the storyteller adds exaggerated or imagined details to it to stress the truth it teaches.

Myth vs. Legend

Can you think of another myth story and another legend story. What is the truth each teaches?

Myth = Tortoise and the Hare
Legend = Johnny Appleseed

A well-known myth

The most famous myth in the Bible is the story of the Fall of the first humans. It seeks to explain that the evil and suffering we now experience had its beginnings in the first humans' choices and in their refusal to trust and obey the laws God gave to guide them to happiness. We need not believe that there was a talking snake, a special tree, or even a special garden. These are symbols to help us understand the deeper truth of original sin, which brought sin into the world.

A well-known legend

An example of a legend in the Bible is the story of Noah. Back in our distant past there was probably some great flood. A man we now call Noah and his family were perhaps able to survive the flood on a boat he had built. He was able to take with him some of the sheep and other animals people raised at that time, so when the flood was over he was able to start over. That much could well be true.

As the story was told over and over, the flood got bigger until it covered all the earth. Noah's boat got bigger. The number of animals he took with him increased to include two of every kind. Those details are imaginative exaggerations, but they help communicate the main point of the story. God is Master of creation and can use natural hardships to allow us to bear the consequences of our sinfulness, but God is also merciful. God's covenant with Noah shows us that God is faithful to those who obey him. If we trust God, he will give us a chance to start over.

So, when you are reading the Bible and come across a story that seems unbelievable, chances are it was never intended by the authors to be believed word for word. It may be a myth, or perhaps a legend. Whichever of the two, these stories are faith stories with deep religious meaning and key religious truths. They are not history. You must always remember to read them as they were intended.

Stranded for Life

If you were going to be stranded on a desert island for the rest of your life, which three books would you take with you? If you did not choose a Bible, why?

Wrap-Up

The goal of this course is to help make the Bible an understood treasure for you. At one level, the Bible contains the history of the Hebrew people, a history that can be divided into logical time periods. On another level, the Bible can seem like a puzzle. Instead of a single book, it is a library of many different kinds of books, writing styles, and topics.

This treasure arrived at its final form by going through three stages of development: from oral tradition to collections of writings to the final editing and arrangement.

Perhaps most important to remember, the Bible was written through hindsight, with new faith insights continually being added throughout the centuries to the old events. As such, the Bible is essentially a faith diary of the Hebrew people. The styles of writings, such as myths and legends, help make this book more of a collection of faith stories than a history book.

Now that you have some of the basic tools needed to uncover the treasure of the Bible, you are ready to begin your expedition.

Check It Out

The Bible was not divided into chapters until the thirteenth century. The chapters were not divided into verses until 1560 C.E.

PRAYER FOR TODAY

Bible Enthronement

Leader: As we begin our study of the Old Testament, we place a Bible in a place of honor as a constant reminder of God's desire to communicate with his people.

(An adaptation of Psalm 50)

Side one: God has spoken to us.

God it is who has summoned us to him.

God it is who has called us from dawn to dusk.

God will not keep silent.

All who are God's servants, God calls.

Side two: Lord, speak your word?

What do you want to say to us?

Side one: Listen, my people, and I will speak.

Side two: I am your God.

I love you very much.

I know well all that has been given to you.

It is your love, your praise, and your thanksgiving that I desire of you.

In turn, I promise you my undying support and love in all your needs.

I will not fail you.

Side one: In turn, what will you choose, my people?

Will you misuse your gift of freedom, to turn away from me?

Will you continue to fail in your love of your brothers and sisters?

Will you also speak words that flow from the shallowness of yourself rather than from the love of your heart?

Side two: Where is your sincerity and truthfulness and love, my people?

I love you so much. Come to me. Do not cut me off from your life.

All: Almighty God , help us listen to your word. In the days ahead, help us observe your faithful presence to your people. Help us understand the lessons from our ancestors about what is possible when we faithfully follow you. Develop in us a deep respect for your word.

Help us apply your word to our own lives.

Amen.

Reflection

Reflection

*"The grass withers, the flower fades;
but the word of our God will stand forever."*
—Isaiah 40:8

1. Identify two ways that the word of God (Bible) is honored at Mass.

2. Is there a way that more respect for the Bible could be given within your home?

HOMEWORK

The following are the names of some of the books in the Bible. Look up in the Bible each book listed below and write what page each book starts and ends on and how many chapters are in each book.

Genesis	1 Kings
Exodus	Psalms
Leviticus	Proverbs
Numbers	Song of Songs
Deuteronomy	Isaiah
Judges	Jeremiah
2 Samuel	Ezekiel

Unscramble the names of the following eight books of the Bible. (Hint: The eight books are found in the above list.)

2

You Shall Be Called Abraham

I will establish my covenant between me and you, and your offspring after you throughout their generations, for an everlasting covenant, to be God to you and to your offspring after you. (Genesis 17:7)

Origin Stories

Read Genesis 11:1–9, a legendary story explaining how all the different languages developed and why. In literature, such stories are called *origin stories.*

Now try your hand at writing an origin story. Choose one of the following titles and develop a story to explain it. Be prepared to share your story with the class.

- How kiwi got to be such a fuzzy, ugly fruit.
- How the elephant got its trunk.
- How the zebra got its stripes.
- How the football got its shape.

Origin story—an account that explains how something began

Setting the scene

The time: about 1750 B.C.E., or almost 4,000 years ago

The place: the Mideast—Iraq, Syria, Palestine, Egypt

The stars: God, and a seventy-five-year-old sheik named Abram and his wife Sarah

The plot: Abram receives God's self-revelation and is invited to join in a **covenant** with God, who promises to make Abram the father of a great nation and to give him a special "promised land."

Covenant—a commitment, promise, or contract between two or more individuals

Who's who?

In addition to Abraham and Sarah, the following is a list of the main people you'll meet in Genesis 12–50.

Lot—Abraham's nephew

Isaac—Abraham and Sarah's only son

Rebekah—wife of Isaac

Jacob (Israel) and Esau—twin sons of Isaac and Rebekah

Rachel and Leah—two wives of Jacob

Laban—father of Rachel and Leah (Jacob's father-in-law)

Joseph—second youngest of Jacob's twelve sons

Jacob's other sons—Leah gave birth to Reuben, Simeon, Levi, Judah, Issachar, and Zebulun. Rachel gave birth to Joseph and Benjamin. Jacob also sired Dan, Naphtali, Gad, and Asher, but the mothers of these sons were servant-girls of his wives

Get Busy!

Draw Abraham and Sarah's family tree.

CATECHISM CLIP

In order to gather together scattered humanity God calls Abram from his country, his kindred, and his father's house, [Gen 12:1.] and makes him Abraham, that is, "the father of a multitude of nations." "In you all the nations of the earth shall be blessed." [Gen 17:5, 12:3 (LXX); cf. Gal 3:8.] (59)

The story in a nutshell

Look how simple the following words from the Bible seem. Yet they contain one of the most important of all God's revelations.

> *Now the LORD said to Abram, "Go from your country and your kindred and your father's house to the land that I will show you. I will make of you a great nation, and I will bless you, and make your name great, so that you will be a blessing. . . ." So Abram went as the LORD had told him. . . .(Genesis 12:1–2, 4)*

What's happening is this: God makes the first move. By this divine self-revelation to Abram, God seeks to establish a friendship with him. As proof of friendship, God promises to give Abram land and make his name famous. Abram, for his part, is asked to trust God completely by letting go of the created things we humans usually depend on for security: family, country, control of our future. Abram agrees. Completely. No hesitation, no questions, no second guessing.

Get Busy!

Write a newspaper article for tomorrow morning's edition relating the story of God and Abraham's actions in Genesis 12:1–9. Make sure you have a catchy headline. You may choose to add an illustration if you have time.

Blind Faith

Has your family ever moved? Have you had to change bedrooms or share your bedroom because of a new baby brother or sister or an older brother or sister leaving home? Have you had to change schools or had a friend move away? How did you feel? What people or things did you miss the most? What was the hardest thing to let go?

Despite various trials and adventures, Abram keeps his promise. So does God. God changes Abram's name to Abraham, meaning the "father of nations." In time, Abraham's grandson, Jacob (also called Israel) has twelve sons. The twelve tribes of Israel descend from this family. Because of a famine, the twelve tribes move from Canaan, the land God gives Abraham, to Egypt around 1500 B.C.E.

Check It Out

God also changed Abraham's wife's name from Sarai to Sarah, which means "princess."

I am called by name

A person's name was very special in ancient times. It was supposed to summarize that person's whole destiny. So when God changed a person's name, as God did with Abraham, Sarah, and Jacob, it meant giving that person a whole new future. We do this, too! Think of times in a person's life when they might change or add to their name. How often does this happen when receiving a sacrament? Do the sacraments have a way of changing our future?

Abram says "YES" "YES"

Think of the relationship you have with your best friend. Do you have a relationship in which you take care of each other, no matter what? It is this kind of commitment that is also reflected in the Hebrew Scripture covenant between God and Abram. Basically, the story of this "friendship" is what we find in chapters 12–50 of the Book of Genesis. Actually, the common thread that runs through the entire Bible comes from this covenant story between God and Abram. All relationships from here on are based on God seeking our friendship and promising to take care of us. In response, we are asked to trust in God to make us happy rather than to rely on created things (which can become **idols** or false gods). That invitation by God is repeated over and over in each new generation of Abram's descendants. Now God offers the invitation to you.

Idol—a person or image offered exceptional attention or devotion

You Are Called. Will You Go?

"I want you to be my friend. I will take care of you always. For your part, I ask you trust in me, listen to my voice and go where I lead you."

Make a list of three things that you would need from God to enable you to trust enough to "give up everything to discover what God has in mind for you."

Father of faith

We have no idea of just how God revealed his message to Abram. The Bible simply says that "God said to Abram . . . " Did God speak in a dream? In a vision? In the secrecy of Abram's heart? We really don't know. This much we do know: Abram had a powerful religious experience where he was convinced that God had spoken to him. So much so that he was willing to give up everything to set out to discover what God had in mind for him. Abram wasn't sure he was capable of the task, but if God thought he could do it, Abram was willing to try.

You Are Ready

Remember a time when someone who is older than you trusted you with a job that they knew you were ready for. What was the job? What were your feelings? Was it pride, or surprise at being considered "old enough," or privileged, or maybe another feeling?

From the moment of that first religious call, Abram, or Abraham, never turned back, never doubted, never stopped trusting in God and in God's promise to him. He was the first to believe in the one true God and he set the pattern for all others who would believe in God—including you! That is why Abraham is called the "father of faith."

What Do You Think?

Do you think it is possible for people your age to have the same kind of faith as Abraham possesses? Why or why not?

A nation that almost wasn't

After Abraham left his homeland, he wandered to Canaan, known today as Israel. There, God revealed that this was to be Abrahm's land, for himself and for his descendants, forever. There was only one problem with this promise. Sarah was barren and Abraham was almost one hundred years old. Abraham surely wondered, "What descendants?" But God promised that Sarah would give him a son, and Abraham never doubted God's promises.

And the promise did come true! A year after a special visit by God, Sarah gave birth to Isaac (Genesis 18). Abraham and Sarah finally had a son, an heir to their kingdom. But the joy of new birth was short lived.

It was a strange religious custom in those days to sacrifice one's firstborn son. Abraham, a religious man, presumed this is what God expected. But if he did sacrifice Isaac, how could he ever have the descendants God kept promising? Once again, Abraham trusted God completely and set out to fulfill the religious custom by sacrificing his son.

God intervened at the last minute and told Abraham that he is not like the other gods. The God of Abraham does not want human sacrifice. Isaac was saved and a nation began (Genesis 22).

Faith to Face Fear

Remember the first time you jumped off the diving board, rode your bike without training wheels, stayed home alone? What did it take for you to let go of your fears and perform the action? Describe your situation and whom you had faith in: yourself, others, God, or all of the above.

Jacob, the trickster

Isaac eventually married and his wife, Rebekah, gave birth to twin sons, Esau and Jacob. While she was pregnant, we get a clue in the Bible that these children will be no ordinary children. God said to her, "Two nations are in your womb, and two peoples born of you shall be divided; the one shall be stronger than the other, the elder shall serve the younger" (Genesis 25:23).

Sure enough, when Rebekah finally gave birth, Jacob, who is born second, came from the womb holding on to his brother Esau's heel (Genesis 25:26). The stage is set for a lifetime of rivalry, much like any rivalry you have with your **siblings**.

Siblings—brothers and sisters

All in the Family? Part 1

Do you get along with your brothers and sisters? Identify two areas of competition or rivalry that exists between you and your siblings.

After the twins grew up, Jacob, with his mother's help, managed to trick Esau out of his **birthright** and his **father's deathbed blessing** by deceiving his old father, Isaac (Genesis 25:29–34 and Genesis 27). This trick was mean enough to cause a great fight between the twins. Actually, Esau threatened to kill Jacob!

Birthright—the privilege that entitled the first-born son to a position of honor in the family and to a double share in the possessions inherited from the father

Deathbed blessing—given by the father to his favorite son at the time of the father's death; the words of the blessing were expected to come true

All In The Family? Part 2

In describing your siblings, what adjectives would you use? Are any smart, or outgoing, or shy, or athletic? Are any of your siblings the favorite of your parents or do you fit into that category? Are you especially close to one of your brothers or sisters?

Jacob's family

Jacob, now the third leader of the chosen people, went to his mother's family to find a wife. This story is just like a modern-day soap opera. Jacob met and fell in love with Rachel at first sight. Rachel's father, Laban, made Jacob work for him for seven years to earn the right to marry Rachel. On the night of the wedding, Laban tricked Jacob into marrying Rachel's elder sister, Leah, instead. The trickster had been tricked! Jacob now had to promise to work another seven years in order to marry Rachel, his true love (Genesis 29).

Get Busy!

Role-play the action that takes place in chapters 27 and 29 of the Book of Genesis.

His wives (and his wives' servant girls) eventually give Jacob twelve sons, and the nation God promised Abraham was well on its way. God's covenant now had extended to the descendants of Abraham, including Jacob—whom God renamed "**Israel**" (Genesis 35:9–15). Jacob and his family became wealthy, powerful, and well-established in Canaan, the promised land. He made peace with his enemies, including Esau and Laban. Life was good.

Check It Out

It was an accepted practice in ancient times for a man to have more than one wife. Large families were necessary for survival in those primitive times, and the quickest way to have a large family was to have several wives. In addition to many wives, men also had children by their female servants, ensuring even more descendants for the man.

Scripture Search

Read Genesis 28. Why do you think God was so opposed to his chosen people marrying outside their group?

What Do You Think?

Do you think God is as present to us today as God seems to have been in the time of Abraham, Isaac, and Jacob? Why or why not?

Israel—one who struggles with God

Joseph

In Jacob's family, most of his sons weren't exactly models of virtue by today's standards, but his favored son, Joseph, was different. And the brothers were jealous of him. As in any family when there is a favorite child, the others, in this case his brothers, become jealous. So the brothers plotted to kill Joseph, but instead, sold him to traders who were on their way to Egypt. To hide their sin, the brothers fool their father, Jacob, by splashing sheep's blood on Joseph's coat and taking it to Jacob, saying that a wild animal killed Joseph (Genesis 37:2–36).

Joseph's story appears to be over, but God has other plans. Joseph was a handsome, intelligent young man with his Great-grandfather Abraham's deep faith in God and a gift for interpreting dreams. His new life in Egypt had many ups and downs. He spent some time in jail, falsely accused of attempted rape. Yet his gift for interpreting dreams eventually gained Pharaoh's attention and got him out of prison. In interpreting the pharaoh's dream, Joseph predicted that Egypt would have seven prosperous years, followed by seven years of severe famine. Pharaoh was impressed and eventually made Joseph his chief assistant, in charge of storing and distributing Egypt's grain (Genesis, chapters 39, 40, 41).

Dream Interpretation— One-on-One Discussion

They say that all of the people and experiences in your dreams are really parts of you and show how you see yourself working through issues in your life. Try to remember one of your dreams and describe it below. In interpreting the dream, what could the feelings, people, struggles, and joys symbolize? Share this dream with a partner and see how they would interpret your dream.

In my dream, I started out for a walk in the forest, but was chased by squirrels. All the sudden I saw a church & ran in it. Out of the blue, I started explaining the theory of relativity. Then I woke up.

Check It Out

Joseph's coat, which made his brothers so jealous (Genesis 37:3), was described as having long sleeves. That was the kind of coat worn only by masters who weren't expected to work. The idea that Jacob regarded Joseph as their master is what really angered the elder brothers.

To Forgive or Not to Forgive

Your best friend says he or she will meet you at the theater to see a movie. He or she never shows up and never explains why. What do you have to gain by forgiving him or her?

Family reunion

The story of Joseph continues as the drought and famine arrive. Because of Joseph's careful planning, Egypt had plenty of grain stored. People from surrounding countries came to Egypt seeking help, including Joseph's brothers. The brothers didn't recognize Joseph, who was now a wealthy and powerful assistant to the pharaoh, but he recognized them. Instead of telling them who he is, Joseph first played tricks on them. (Remember, they tried to kill him!) Joseph especially wanted to be sure they've repented their past crime (Genesis 42–45). Could you be so forgiving if your siblings tried to kill you? What faith Joseph had!

Eventually Joseph revealed his true identity, and there was great rejoicing all around. Joseph used his influence with the pharaoh and arranged to have his father and brothers move to Egypt. They were given prime land for their herds and, under Joseph's special protection, they prospered.

Now all the descendants of Abraham were living in Egypt. This set the stage for the development of the Exodus story and the next book of the Bible, Exodus.

To Do at Home

Taking the story of Joseph, draw a cartoon strip depicting all of the events of his life. Then you decide if he was a superhero!

Scripture Search

Read Genesis 22.

1. Do you think God sometimes tests people's faith today? How?

____

____

____

____

2. Has God ever tested your faith?

____

____

____

____

Some key faith lessons

As we said before, if you are looking for the common thread that runs through the Bible, this is it: God seeks our friendship and promises to take care of us. In response, we are asked to trust in God to make us happy rather than to rely on created things, which can become idols or false gods. This is the greatest faith lesson to learn from the Bible.

A second key lesson that emerges is this: God isn't bound by human rules. For example, in ancient times the eldest son was supposed to become the chief heir and head of the family, but God chose Jacob over his older brother, Esau. God also chose Joseph instead of Jacob's oldest son, Rueben. You'll see God breaking our "human rules" over and over throughout the Scriptures.

There's a third faith lesson to note. God can take our sins and failures and turn them to his advantage. God won't take away our freedom. Even when we use it badly, God's plan still is achieved. The main example of this is the story of Joseph. What Joseph's brothers did to him was terrible. God was able to turn this sin into a means of saving the children of Abraham. So God's purpose is achieved, and God's promise to us is kept even if it's done with many struggles throughout the process.

prayer = talking to God
formal - MASS - highest
personal - personal

Reflection

To you, O LORD, I lift up my soul. . . .
Make me to know your ways, O LORD;
teach me your paths.
Lead me in your truth, and teach me, for you are the God of my salvation;
for you I wait all day long. (Psalm 25:1, 4–5)

1. Do you take enough time to lift up your soul to God in prayer?

sometimes

2. How do you think God seeks to teach and guide you?

yes, each & every day.

3. What do you think is the most important thing God has taught you so far in your life?

patience

PRAYER FOR TODAY

Leader: Through his ability to interpret dreams, Joseph earned fame and a position of leadership. How much attention do we pay to our dreams and our urgings? Are they whispers from God?

Side one: I am told that there are folks who refuse to dream because their dreams have been so seemingly shattered, like dreams that die at birth. And so they hide their dreams in small corners of their hearts and pretend they aren't there.

Side two: But as for me, I am almost sure that in the Body of Christ that we call the Church, we have the power to help each other's dream come true. For in the dark moments when light has hidden its face for a while, we are the stars meant to shine for each other and we do!

Side one: More than anything else I would like to remind you that dreams hidden within you have the power to become a gospel.

Side two: And it is important for you to know that as it is for the sun to shine or the rain to fall or a heart to beat, because only if we believe in the gospel that lives inside those hidden dreams in us can the strangers we walk with afford to dream.

All: God, as we continue to listen for your voice and to learn to trust you, help us be open to the many ways you share yourself with us. Amen.

—Author and publisher unknown

HOMEWORK

Chapter 2 Word Search

Abram
Asher
Benjamin
Bible
birthright
book
called
Canaan
coat
covenant
Dan
deathbed blessing
descendants
dream
Esau
Egypt
families
father of faith
Gad
Genesis
God
Hagar
idol
Isaac
Ishmael
Israel
Issachar
Jacob
Joseph
Judah
Laban
Leah
Levi
Lot
Mideast
Naphtali
origin
pharaoh
promised land
Rachel
Rebekah
Reuben
revelation
Sarah
servants
sheik
sibling
Simeon
sons
stories
tribes
wives
Zebulun

Z I S A A C J H T N A N E V O C O V B N Q
D E L L A C N S A Y S E I L I M A F A U U
E J U D A H A E W K G T K P S U L A D L I
T G C J W E D R L E E A R O S N N T K U G
S T N A D N E C S E D B M A A A A H R B T
A S H I P H R B I B L E E B C I V E Y E K
E O M T S U N D S F T X I R H L F R T Z T
D R E A I S O N S I L F Q M A A S O A M P
I I T S B L E A M H S I A A R T L F R K Y
M G H N L Q M L E A H E G E N H H F T S G
P I G A I V I D B W R I N A R P R A H T E
S N I B N L S E O D R E V E L A T I O N S
G E R A G E N S O J E R U E G N C T A K H
A N H L B J V I K U E B A A L D O H R W E
D E T I A A C M A S E R H M B Q A M A R I
U S R M B C K O A N S C O T G R T P H E K
B T I X Z O R R F I D O G J A I A M P W L
O N B C R B A P M V S T O R I E S M P E J
S E V I W H R G H P E S O J H K D V R O M

3

Passover, Exodus, and Covenant

"I am the LORD your God, who brought you out of the land of Egypt, out of the house of slavery; you shall have no other gods before me." (Exodus 20:2–3)

Thou shalt . . . small-group work

Instructions: Read the account of Moses receiving the Ten Commandments in chapter 20 in the Book of Exodus. Now, with your group, develop a set of "ten commandments" for one of the following choices:

- Ten commandments for being good friends
- Ten commandments for being good athletes
- Ten commandments for being good students
- Ten commandments for being good musicians
- Ten commandments for being good artists

Share your group's work with the other groups.

Setting the scene

The time: from about 1250 B.C.E. to approximately 1200 B.C.E.

The place: northern Egypt, the most powerful and advanced civilization of the day, and the Sinai Peninsula, a vast, arid, desert region to the east

The plot: The Israelites, welcomed into Egypt in the time of Joseph, had become slaves and had been forced to work on the pharaoh's vast building projects. God, remembering the promise made to Abraham and his descendants, calls Moses to free the chosen people. Aided by powerful acts of God (the plagues, the Passover event, the parting of the Red Sea), the Israelites make good their exodus from Egypt into the Sinai Desert. There, God forms an official covenant with the people at Mount Sinai. The people, out of fear and uncertainty, respond to God by complaining, and they sin against God. For this, they must wander forty years in the desert before they arrive at the borders of Canaan, their homeland. It is at this border that they prepare to invade the land occupied by the Canaanites and other tribes.

Attitude Breeds Success

As you have probably discovered, attitude is everything when it comes to accomplishing a task. Most "winners" tell you that skill is only part of the reason for their win. Can you think of a time when your attitude hurt your chances at "winning" or completing something? How about a time when your attitude brought you success?

Who's who?

The following are some of the key people found in the story of the Passover.

Moses—the most famous hero of this period of Israelite history

Zipporah—the wife of Moses

Jethro—Zipporah's father, Moses' father-in-law

Aaron—Moses' brother and chief assistant

Joshua and Caleb—Moses' military leaders

Pharaoh—the leader of Egypt

Check It Out

The word *el* in Hebrew means "god." Abraham called God "El Shaddai," meaning "God Almighty." *Jehovah* is the name for God found in some translations of the Bible. It is actually a mistranslation of YHWH or Yahweh.

The Bible account

Even though we're focusing on a rather short period of time (fifty years to be precise), this is the core story of the entire history of Israel. Everything that happens to Israel after this event is viewed, by hindsight, in light of these events. There are four books of the Bible devoted to telling this story: Exodus, Leviticus, Numbers, and Deuteronomy. For many reasons, these are considered the most important books in the Hebrew Scriptures.

Remember how we said that the final version of the Bible we have today is an edited account that combines many different versions and interpretations of the original events? Well, in these four books, you'll see plenty of cases where the editors keep two or more versions of the same event. The call of Moses is a good example.

Scripture Search

Read Exodus 3:1–6 and Exodus 6:2–12 and compare the two stories. In what ways are they the same? Different?

____

____

____

The Power of God

Can you identify three events of nature that you feel are the direct result of God's plan of creation?

____

____

____

A drama in three acts

The first act in the story focuses on how God, through the leadership of Moses, helps the **Israelites** escape from Egypt in what is called the *Passover event*. Basically, God makes Pharaoh "an offer he can't refuse."

Check It Out

The children of Abraham came to be called *Israelites* because they are descendants of the sons of Israel. The Israelites were called *Hebrews* (possibly from *habiru*) by the Egyptians. It meant "Semite" or "people from the East." The Romans began to call the Israelites *Judaei* after the tribe of Judah. The modern term *Jew* is a variation of *Judaei*, or children of Judah.

In the story of the **Passover**, God demonstrates clearly that no other gods, even the gods of the powerful Egyptians, can hold a candle to the God of Abraham, Isaac, and Jacob. The strength of God is shown through the ten plagues and culminates in the Passover event. The parting of the Red Sea confirms to the Israelites how God will take care of them as the Israelites pass safely through the Red Sea and the Egyptian army drowns. Lastly, manna and quail are provided in the desert to convincingly prove God's love.

Passover—a Jewish religious feast held in remembrance of God saving the chosen people from the tenth plague

All these wonders set the stage for the second act. Once it is clear that their God is for real and totally committed to them, the Israelites are asked to entrust themselves to that God in a permanent, formal covenant. They are chosen as God's special people; therefore, they are expected to act that way.

The third act focuses on the Israelites' wanderings and adventures in the desert. It tells how the Israelites had to struggle to learn how to live up to the covenant. Despite all that God had already done for them, they often wavered in their faith. Moses called them a "stiff-necked" people and wanted to give up on them.

Check It Out

The forty days of Lent we celebrate each year are intended to be a desert experience, recalling the "forty years" the Israelites wandered in the desert while being purified and drawing closer to God.

Trust Walk—small group

In a group of five, choose one person to be a leader. The other four people are blindfolded. Holding onto each other's shoulders, the leader directs the rest of the group around an assigned path. The leader must direct his group over or around barriers that are located on the path. Which group can complete the path the quickest and with the fewest accidents?

1. What fear did you have if you were one of the blindfolded people?

2. What responsibility did you feel if you were the leader?

3. What problems did your group experience?

4. What similar problems do you think Moses and the Israelites experienced?

The call and mission of Moses

The story begins when God called Moses, who was wanted for murder in Egypt and was hiding out in Midian (Exodus 2:11–3:20). There, God revealed to Moses, through a burning bush, God's desire for Moses to lead the chosen people out of Egypt.

Despite this wonderful experience at the burning bush, Moses was not overjoyed with what God was asking him to do. Moses was to go to the court of Pharaoh, the most powerful ruler in the world at that time, and tell him to let the Israelite slaves go free. Moses probably thought to himself, "You've got to be kidding." God assured Moses that Moses would have special powers and that God would actually be the one doing the convincing.

Moses Lives!

Imagine you are Moses. What would you prepare to say to the pharaoh when you meet with him?

Things didn't go well at first. Pharaoh ignored Moses. He even punished the Israelites with more work for less food. This got the Israelites angry at Moses, but Moses, with God's prodding, hung in there. Finally, things began to move into high gear. (Exodus 5)

CATECHISM CLIP

God, our Creator and Redeemer, chose Israel for himself to be his people and revealed his Law to them, thus preparing for the coming of Christ. The Law of Moses expresses many truths naturally accessible to reason. These are stated and authenticated within the covenant of salvation. (1961)

The plagues

God told Moses to threaten the Egyptians with a series of plagues if Pharaoh didn't cooperate. Pharaoh ignored the threats, and the plagues began to happen, just as Moses predicted.

Plagues—disease, troubles, or afflictions that affect a large number of people

It's possible, of course, to explain the plagues partly as natural events. For example, the Nile became choked with red, blood-like mud because of rain upriver. This drove the frogs out of the water where they died, breeding gnats and flies that fed on them—and on the people. These gnat and fly bites caused infections, leading to boils. And the darkness possibly resulted from volcanic ash in the air after a major eruption that archaeologists say took place in the Mideast about that time. And, of course, hail and locusts are occurrences.

Does this take away the miraculous meaning of these plagues? Not really. Remember, the God of Abraham is the Creator and Ruler of all of nature. When these plagues happened as Moses predicted, the Israelites believed it was God's doing, even though the events themselves were natural enough. Unfortunately for Pharaoh and the Egyptians, they didn't see it that way. Despite all these plagues, Pharaoh refused to let the Israelites go.

Scripture Search

Read Exodus chapters 7–11. Imagine that Moses is appealing to the pharaoh who is living in today's world. Design and draw ten plagues that could occur today. Remember, they have to be natural occurrences and there has to be a possibility that they could really happen.

Check It Out

The Passover experience was also called the *Pasch* by the Israelites. The Pasch was their major feast each year. The name *Pascal Mystery*, which is central to our Christian faith, has its roots in this same Passover, or Pasch.

Change Your Mind ? ? ?

How many times in a day would you guess you change your mind about things? Are you someone who is known for changing your mind? What does this do for you? For others?

Passover and Exodus

The pharaoh's stubbornness led to the final plague. God told Moses to predict to Pharaoh the sudden death of all firstborn Egyptian males in the land. God also told Moses to instruct the Israelite people on how to protect their sons from this plague. God's angel of death would "pass over" the Israelites and strike the Egyptians. This preparation included painting the doorposts with lambs' blood and then eating a special religious meal. Moses instructed the Israelites to be ready to leave Egypt as soon as the signal sounded.

God struck the Egyptians and "passed over" the Israelites, and Pharaoh finally had enough. He admitted defeat when his own son died. He finally allowed the Israelites to leave. God rescued the people as Moses had promised!

The Israelites left, but Pharaoh changed his mind and pursued them. The Israelites seemed trapped at the edge of the Red Sea, but the sea parted at the command of Moses and the Israelites passed through. Pharaoh's army followed, but the sea flowed back and engulfed them. The Israelites were safe—and free! We could probably partly explain this event with natural causes. No matter. In faith, the Israelites knew it was God who had destroyed the Egyptian army and brought them to safety on the other side of the sea.

The Covenant

The Israelites headed south into the Sinai Peninsula. This is a desert with a capital "D." It suddenly dawned on the happy ex-slaves that they were going to need food and water. God provided them with the mysterious **manna** and then with quail and water (Exodus 16:1–16).

After wandering for about three months, the Israelites ended up at the foot of Mount Sinai at the southern end of the desert. There, God summoned Moses to the top of the mount and revealed the covenant, a pact God wished to make with the children of Abraham, through the tablets of the Ten Commandments.

Manna—quite possibly the edible, white substance produced by beetles still found in the Sinai Desert today. It has a slightly sweet taste and is quite nourishing.

Scripture Search

Read Exodus 16:1–17:7. Why do you think God would not allow the Israelites to collect more than one day's supply of manna at a time?

View from Mt. Sinai

A Relationship of Real Commitment

A covenant relationship is a pact of love between two or more people. This pact includes an agreement by both parties to do for the other, as long as they do for you. It's similar to a contract where you agree to provide a service for someone for payment or for a similar service in return. List a covenant you have with each of the following people or groups. For example, with your parents, if you do your household chores, you get your weekly allowance.

Parents ______________________________

____

Family ______________________________

____

Friends ______________________________

____

Teacher ______________________________

____

God ______________________________

____

Abraham's covenant is a two-way commitment. God claimed the Israelites as the chosen people, who belong to the God who rescued them. Having demonstrated the power of the one true God, their God promised to stay with the Israelites, to protect them and to care for them.

For their part, the Israelites had two basic tasks. First, they were to continue to trust in God above all else. They were not to look to other gods for protection. Second, they were to treat one another fairly and justly, just as God treated them. This meant being truthful, respecting the life and property of others, caring for their parents, and avoiding adultery. This especially meant caring for those who were weak, poor, and strangers and who couldn't care for themselves. Do these tasks sound like the Ten Commandments? Well, they are!

The Ten "Dos" rather than the Ten "Don'ts"—small group

In a small group, rewrite the Ten Commandments using modern language and stating positive requests rather than the negative commands given to us in the biblical version. Then discuss if changing the language changes the message or the power behind the message.

But even as God was explaining all this to Moses on Mount Sinai, the Israelites were being unfaithful. Aaron, of all people, helped the group make a golden calf that they wanted to worship as their new god or as a forbidden image of God. Just as the celebration was getting under way, Moses returned with the covenant. Needless to say, both he and God were very angry. (Read Exodus 32.)

The people repented and were given a second chance. God called Moses back up the mountain and again wrote the covenant. This time the people waited for Moses and they agreed to the covenant Moses presented to them. Then God sent them forth toward Canaan, the land of their ancestors, Abraham and Sarah.

A Covenant Broken

You just identified several covenant relationships of our time. What would happen if one side of the covenant would not follow through with their side of the bargain? What does this do to the trust in the relationship?

Check It Out

Tradition tells us that the place where God first appeared to Moses in the burning bush is near Mount Sinai, where God later revealed the covenant to the Israelites. Mount Sinai is also referred to as Mount Horeb in the Bible.

Desert wandering

The Bible says it took the Israelites forty years to reach Canaan. This was not because it was that far nor because they didn't know the way. In fact, they came right to the border not too long after the covenant experience, but they lost courage. They doubted that the God who had just rescued them from Egypt and provided them with food and water in a barren desert would help them settle in the land of the Canaanites.

That is when God decided that none of those who had escaped from Egypt would be allowed to enter the promised land. That privilege would be reserved for their children. The two exceptions were Joshua and Caleb, who had never doubted. (Read about it in Numbers, chapter 14.)

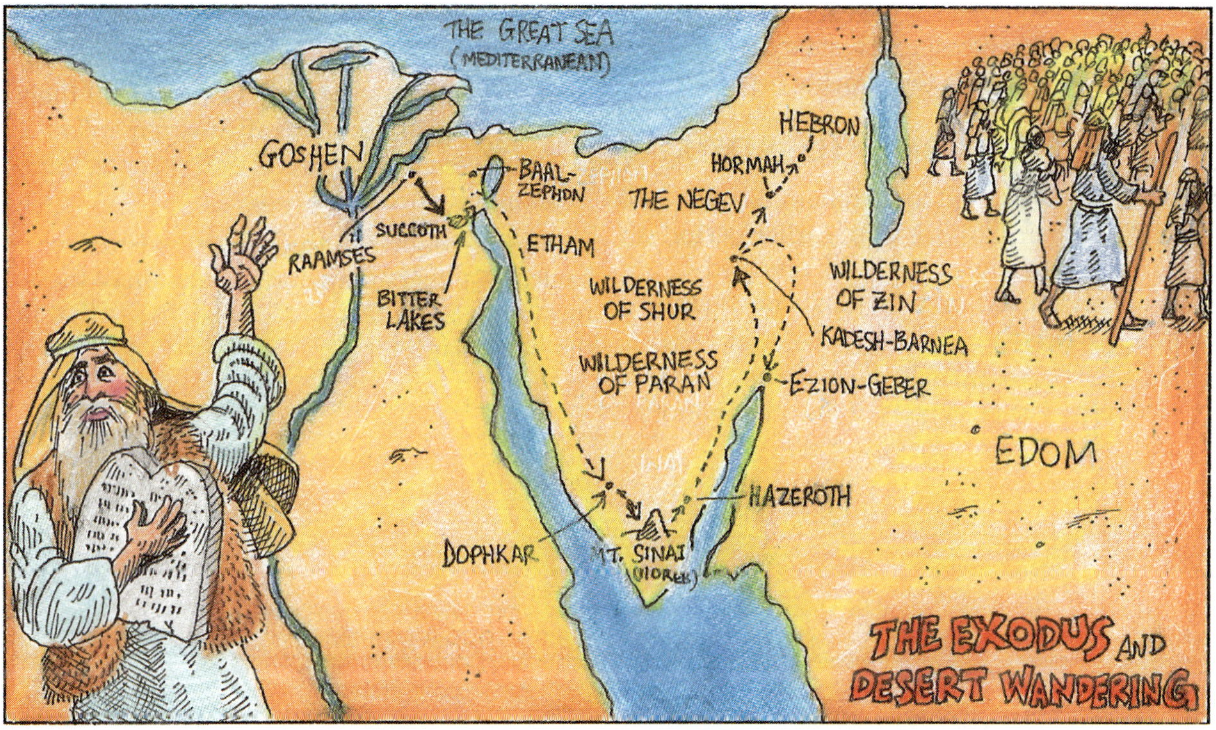

Circle of Trust

Form a circle of eight to ten people who stand shoulder to shoulder. One person stands in the middle and with his or her eyes closed, stiffly falls to the outside of the circle. Those in the circle must catch the middle person and push him or her to another person. Assure the person in the middle that the circle will not let him or her fall.

If you were the person in the middle, what fears did you have?

What did it take for you to *not* doubt that you would fall?

Did you lose trust and open your eyes?

If you were a person in the circle, what responsibilities did you feel?

How does this exercise relate to what the Israelites were experiencing?

The Israelites headed back into the desert. As they wandered during those years, they repeatedly broke the covenant they had made with God. They often rebelled. They wavered in their trust in God and God's power. They grumbled and complained like spoiled children. Even Moses wavered in faith once and paid for it by not being allowed to enter the promised land (Numbers 20:1–13).

The story ends with the Israelites poised on the borders of Canaan, ready to advance. Moses gave them final instructions about their covenant and his blessing. Then he died, and a new chapter begins in the Israelite history.

Some key faith lessons

What God revealed to Abraham, Isaac, Jacob, and their families in an earlier period in a kind of sketchy way now was revealed clearly and backed up with God's powerful, wonderful acts.

1. The God of Abraham is the one true God of all that is. The false gods of the other nations are just that: false and powerless.
2. The God of Abraham is a saving, freeing, life-giving God.
3. Their God is faithful, a God who seals his promises in a special covenant with the people. Even while punishing their infidelities, God remains faithful, always willing to receive them back if they seek forgiveness.
4. The people have responsibilities, too, as God's chosen people. They must continue to trust in him above all else, rather than turning to false gods or relying on earthly wealth and power as the other nations do.
5. The Passover experience is the core of their faith life. They were to always remember it. They were to celebrate it each year as their main religious feast.

All that follows in the history of Israel is basically a deepening and expansion of these fundamental beliefs. We'll begin to see that in the next chapter.

Part of Our Roots

Read Exodus 12. Name elements of our Eucharist that have their roots in the Passover as described in this chapter.

1. Sacrificed lamb
2. Unleavened bread
3. Solemn assembly

Think About It

Why do you think the Israelites had such a hard time learning to trust in God? Do you think it is easier to learn to trust in God today? Why or why not?

____

____

____

Wrap-Up

We've just viewed the three acts of the Exodus drama. God called Moses, worked wonderful miracles, and freed the Israelites. In the desert, God formed a covenant with the people. It took about forty years of wandering in the desert for the meaning and responsibilities of that covenant to begin to sink in. It will take you some time to come to a clearer understanding of what all this will mean in your faith life, too. Meanwhile, be sure to read the various passages suggested—with eyes of faith.

Reflection

But Moses said to God, "If I come to the Israelites and say to them, 'The God of your ancestors has sent me to you,' and they ask me, 'What is his name?' what shall I say to them?" God said to Moses, "I AM WHO I AM." He said further,"Thus you shall say to the Israelites, 'I AM has sent me to you.'" (Exodus 3:13–14)

To know a person's name indicated a familiarity and equality with that person. This is why it was important for Moses and the Israelites to know God's name. God gave Moses a strong indication of the kind of relationship God wanted with the Israelites when he said his name was "I AM." What kind of relationship does God desire with all of us based on the following reflection on God's name?

I was regretting the past and fearing the future.
Suddenly God spoke: "My name is I AM."
God paused. I waited.
God continued, "When you live in the past with its mistakes and regrets, it is hard.
I am not there. My name is not I WAS.
When you live in the future, with its problems and fears, it is hard.
I am not there. My name is not I WILL BE.
When you live in this moment, it is not hard, I am here.
My name is I AM."

—*Helen Mallicoat*

PRAYER FOR TODAY

Leader: The journey of the Israelite people is our journey also when we set out to follow the Lord.

Side one: God continually made known to the Israelites that he wanted them to be God's people. Over and over, God had to reassure them that he would take care of them if they but trusted him. They would follow for a while, then go their own way until there was no other choice but to turn back to God.

Side two: Because they did not trust completely, their journey took a lot longer than it should have. They could have walked straight into the promised land, but instead they gave into temptation and went their own direction.

Side one: God promises us complete happiness also; all we need to do is to follow him. But we, too, give into the temptations around us that keep us from trusting in this God who offers us unconditional love in return for complete belief in him. We listen to the voices on television and in the newspapers that say we will find complete happiness if we buy this toy or attend this event. And so our journey takes longer than it needs, too.

Side two: But God's promise stays constant: follow me and I will show you the way. I will give you all you need to survive and be happy. "But strive first for the kingdom of God and his righteousness, and all these things will be given to you as well" (Matthew 6:33).

All: Loving God, as you walk with me in the events of my days, help me be constantly aware of your loving presence. Show me your way and give me the strength to trust and believe in you. Assist me in keeping my part in my convenant of faith begun at my baptism. Let me be quick to ask forgiveness when I fail so that I may soon return to the path that leads to your protection and love. Amen.

HOMEWORK

Bible Search Activity

At the Seder meal, the youngest child asks four questions that help the people understand the meaning of the Passover. Find the answers to these four questions in Exodus, chapters 12 and 13.

1. Why is this night different from all other nights?

2. Why do we eat only unleavened bread?

3. Why do we eat bitter herbs and haroset?

4. Why on this night do we celebrate the Passover?

4

From Judges to Kings

"We came to the land to which you sent us; it flows with milk and honey, and this is its fruit."
(Numbers 13:27)

Imagine This—small group work

The people come to you and ask you to be their ruler. Because you want to be a good ruler, you make five promises regarding what you will do as their ruler. Write your promises below.

1.

2.

3.

4.

5.

See how your promises compare to those developed by the others in your group.

Setting the scene

The time: the period from 1200 B.C.E. to 970 B.C.E.

The place: Canaan, the land on the east coast of the Mediterranean Sea, now called Israel and Palestine

The plot: The Israelites, after forty years of wandering in the Sinai Desert, finally invade and take possession of Canaan, the land God promised to Abraham and his descendants. They divide into twelve tribes and settle in the territories assigned to them. A series of judges govern the people in God's name until the Israelites ask for a king to rule them. Saul becomes their first king in 1030 B.C.E. Civil war breaks out in this first united kingdom governed by Saul. David replaces Saul as king in 1010 B.C.E., eventually bringing peace and unity to the land. David rules until 970 B.C.E. After he dies, his son, Solomon, becomes king.

Leadership Qualities

If you could choose the leader of the land you were living in, what qualities would you want him or her to have?

Reclaiming the promised land

When the Israelites reached the border of Canaan around 1200 B.C.E., they did not find a "Welcome Home" sign greeting them. The land had been occupied for several centuries by Canaanites and others who did not care who promised whom the land they now considered theirs. They were ready to fight. Behind the walls of Jericho, they held their ground.

With the powerful help of the chosen people's God, Joshua eventually conquered the Canaanites and settled the tribes in various parts of the land. In all, it took about fifty years before Israel's tribes could say they were at home. Many of the previous inhabitants of Canaan continued to live there and began to learn the laws and the rituals of the Israelites.

Who's who?

A number of famous Old Testament figures, some of whom you may be familiar with, lived during this period. They include the following:

Joshua—Moses' second-in-command who became the leader of the Israelites after the death of Moses. A wise and holy man, he was also a great military leader who guided the Israelites in the invasion and conquest of Canaan.

Deborah, Gideon, Samson—some of the more famous of the judges who governed the Israelites after the death of Joshua

Ruth—great-grandmother of David. The Book of Ruth tells her story.

Samuel—priest and prophet who served as leader of Israel, bridging the period between the last judge, Eli, and King Saul, whom Samuel anointed. Samuel later rejected Saul and anointed David as king to replace Saul.

Saul—a tragic figure and first king of Israel, who ruled from 1030 to 1010 B.C.E.

David—ranks with Abraham and Moses as one of the greatest persons of the Old Testament

Jonathan—son of Saul, close friend of David

Nathan—prophet and advisor to David

Joab—one of David's best, most loyal military leaders

Absalom—one of David's sons who led a rebellion against his father

Bathsheba—wife of Uriah and David. David married Bathsheba after he arranged to have Uriah killed in battle. She is the mother of Solomon.

Abraham → Moses → David

God!

Draw a picture of what you believe God looks like. Write three complete sentences that describe or explain your picture.

The period after the Exodus was a period of war and conquest. God often appears in the Book of Joshua as a kind of war-God, cruel and merciless to the enemies of the chosen people. As you read this part of the Old Testament, keep in mind the Israelites' understanding of God was still quite undeveloped at this time. A more tender understanding of God's justice and mercy and God's love for all people develops later in their history.

CATECHISM CLIP

The first commandment forbids honoring gods other than the one Lord who has revealed himself to his people. It proscribes superstition and irreligion. Superstition in some sense represents a perverse excess of religion; irreligion is the vice contrary by defect to the virtue of religion. (2110)

Check It Out

The Israelites, who had been nomads and shepherds, first learned farming from the Canaanites whom they conquered. As farmers, the Canaanites worshiped gods called *baals*, who were primarily fertility gods. As the Israelites became farmers, they were often tempted to forget God's first commandment, "I am the LORD your God, who brought you out of the land of Egypt, out of the house of slavery; you shall have no other gods before me" (Exodus 20:2–3). Eventually, they fell back to their old ways and honored the Canaanites' baals.

Not exactly a model federation

The twelve tribes formed a kind of federation, which is a union of separate groups with one leadership. Despite their separateness, the thread of their common history and their common covenant with God was the uniting factor that kept them together. This thread was strong for a while, but it eventually became weak with jealousies, self-interest, and disputes over the boundaries of their territories. This led to bickering and fighting among the tribes. On occasion, some tribes even made alliances with the tribes that remained in the area (or later invaded it) and fought against other tribes of Israel.

The federation was the only form of government uniting the twelve tribes. God was considered their leader and the covenant was considered their common law. The judges of each tribe did provide a loosely organized leadership. Keep in mind these "**judges**" weren't judges in the legal sense that we think of today. Rather, they were wise and gifted leaders called forth by God and recognized by all the tribes.

Judge—someone recognized as wise and gifted and called by God

Two famous judges were Deborah (Judges 4–5) and Gideon (Judges 6–9), but perhaps the most famous of the judges was Samson, a great military leader known for his physical strength. A well-known story about Samson was his forbidden love for the non-Israelite Delilah, which finally did him in, though not before he repented his sin and rescued his people (Judges 13–16).

Our Personal Judges

Referring to the Old Testament definition of judge, who do you know today who would fit this definition? Why?

____

____

____

____

Overall, the period of the judges (from about 1200 to 1030 B.C.E.) was not a happy time for the Israelites. Again, the Israelites continually broke God's covenant and they were punished for it. They were constantly fighting against themselves and their enemies, such as the Philistines, who began to invade Canaan around 1150 B.C.E. For all these reasons, the people came to the judge Samuel and asked him to speak to God about giving them a king who could lead them and defend them against these powerful enemies (1 Samuel 8:4–5).

Fighting to Be Christian

The Israelites were constantly being led astray by the peoples living among them. Do we have a similar problem trying to be good Catholic Christians while living in a society that contradicts our Christian values? If your life were a movie, how would those watching it know you were a Christian?

____

____

____

____

____

Check It Out

The Philistines, who gave the Israelites such a hard time, brought with them a new development: iron weapons. These were stronger than the old-fashioned bronze weapons of the Israelites. The name *Palestine* is actually a variation of Philistine.

Give us a king like the other nations

God opposed the idea of giving the Israelites a king. In a real sense, by asking for a king, they were rejecting God's leadership over them. God tried to warn them that a king would have absolute rule over them and that they wouldn't like it.

False Gods

If the king was considered a "false god" who could pull people away from the God of Abraham, then what in our time could be considered a power that pulls us away from God's leadership in our lives? What is it in our society that pulls us away from our Christian values?

But the people insisted. Finally, God agreed and sent Samuel to anoint Saul, a member of the tribe of Benjamin, as their king. From the very beginning, some of the people didn't like the idea of Saul as their king (1 Samuel 10:25–27).

Saul began his reign as king pretty smoothly. He won several battles against Israel's enemies, but he wasn't bringing unity to the tribes. Saul began to lose control as he personally suffered from some form of mental illness. He had terrible headaches; he broke into fits of rage and jealousy; he became cruel and vengeful. Much of this rage and jealousy was directed against David, as we'll see in a minute. Worst of all, he began to break the covenant.

Power Corrupts

Sometimes, when a person takes on a leadership role, their greed for power or control makes them do things that aren't good. Can you think of three leaders (either political, sports, or entertainment) that have somehow fallen into this trap?

You have to realize that the main task of the king, in God's mind, was to serve as the people's religious leader and to ensure that the people remained faithful to the covenant, the real law for Israel. He was also to protect the poor, the helpless, and all the people from the surrounding pagan tribes, who could lead the Israelites into idol worship. So when a king broke the covenant himself, he went against the very purpose of his kingship. That's what ultimately led God to reject Saul and choose David.

Scripture Search

Read 1 Samuel 8:1–20.

1. Why do you think the people wanted a king? Did it show a lack of faith?

2. Could God complain about you the same way God complained about the Israelites in verses 7–9?

David and Saul

After Saul was rejected (though he still ruled as king), God sent Samuel to anoint David, the youngest son of Jesse, to be the next king. David, in his teens at the time, was a handsome, talented youth working as a shepherd for his father.

Although anointed by Samuel, David didn't automatically become king. Saul was still in charge. David served in Saul's court and soon became Saul's favorite. He was a talented harpist and poet and seemed to be the only one who could give Saul any relief when he suffered his headaches and attacks of sadness (1 Samuel 16).

A Real Leader

David's qualities of being handsome, athletic, a musician and a poet gained him acceptance as a king. Is there anyone in today's world—man or woman—who has this combination of qualities? What do you believe are the top five qualities a leader should possess? Do the people you mentioned above also possess the qualities you listed?

David quickly became a national hero when he saved Israel by killing Goliath. David's instant fame and popularity caused Saul to become jealous. Saul began to plot to have David killed by sending him on dangerous missions against the Philistines. Yet each time, David came back victorious and his fame became greater than ever. Once, in a fit of rage, Saul even tried to kill David right in his own court.

Saul eventually commited suicide after losing a battle against the Philistines. The way was now clear for David to become king.

Scripture Search

Read 1 Samuel 17:4, 32–51.

What other legend or tale, where the unlikely person is victorious, does this remind you of? What do you think is the real lesson contained in the story of David and Goliath? Does it have any application to your own life?

____

____

____

____

____

David, king of contradictions

On one hand, David was able to do what Saul failed to do. He eventually succeeded in uniting all the tribes behind him, in subduing all the neighboring enemy tribes, and in setting up Jerusalem as both the religious and political capital of the kingdom. On the other hand, he had his own share of troubles, many of which he brought on himself. In the end, he called the people back into fidelity with God. With this, David became Israel's greatest king and his reign became the model against which all later kings are judged.

Check It Out

The city of Jerusalem is built on a mount almost exactly in the center of the land of Canaan, which the Israelites captured. David realized it made an ideal capital from which to rule all the tribes. Jerusalem means "city of peace."

On the personal level, David was a bundle of contradictions. He was a great military leader; he was a poet and musician; he was deeply religious and devout; and he was fiercely loyal to his friends. In contradiction, he could be vain and proud; he was an adulterer; he was a murderer, who betrayed one of his most loyal generals, Uriah, to marry Uriah's wife, Bathsheba (2 Samuel 11–12).

With all of these contradictions, you'd hardly think David would have become a model and one of the great heroes of Israel. God would certainly reject David as God had rejected Saul. Wrong! David listened to his advisors when they pointed out his sins and David was able to admit those sins and seek forgiveness. He made amends for all his sins and never once did he waver in his love and loyalty to God and God's covenant.

Curious people want to know!

Choosing from the many stories of David found in 1 and 2 Samuel, create a ten-week television series that highlights David's life. Which stories do you think the viewers of today would find most interesting? Which stories are necessary for understanding the story of what happens next? Would David be depicted as a hero or villain for today's people?

Relationships

Like David, how do you use forgiveness to make your relationship with your parents better? Describe the situation and the end result.

So the relationship between God and David continued despite the contradictions. In fact, God even renewed with David the covenant once made with Abraham. Along with the agreement, God made a promise for one of David's ancestors (Jesus, as it turns out) to eventually become the King of kings who would rule an everlasting kingdom. This additional promise gave the Israelites hope to withstand any problems that would arise, from the time of David even to now.

At the time of David's death, the twelve tribes of Israel had become a peaceful and prosperous kingdom, loyal to God, to the king, and to the covenant. David's son Solomon, noted for his wisdom, assumed the throne. For a while things were good, yet this golden age would not last long.

Check It Out

For a long time it was thought that all the psalms were written by David. Though this is not true, David did write a number of the psalms, many dealing with his struggles with his enemies while he was king (for example, read Psalm 13).

Key faith lessons

During this period of the conquest, several key faith themes became more and more clear to Israel.

1. The promise God made to Abraham was kept and Abraham's "children" were brought back to the promised land.
2. God's purpose was achieved despite all human odds against it, because God was more powerful than any army.
3. It was better to trust in God than to rely on kings, military power, and wealth, the way other nations do.
4. Israel's peace and happiness always came from loyalty to the God of Abraham and the covenant, not from the size of its armies nor its treasury.
5. Israel could expect trouble every time it ignored the covenant and slipped into idolatry, selfishness, or injustice.

As we'll see, these basic lessons will be repeated throughout the Hebrew Scriptures until the time of Jesus. Speaking of Jesus, it is also during this time that the seeds are first planted for Israel's expectation of a messiah, a son of David who will establish an everlasting kingdom of peace and justice.

Wrap-Up

The key events of this period seem simple enough. Israel conquered Canaan and settled in Canaan. For a time, the tribes lived as a kind of federation, governed by judges and the covenant until it became a well-established kingdom in that area.

Yet it wasn't that simple. Israel continued to be surrounded by enemies and new ones kept showing up. Worse, many other groups continued to live side-by-side with the Israelites, influencing them away from the covenant into other religious practices contrary to their belief in one God. Finally, even though Israel was a united kingdom, the unity wasn't very strong. The individual tribes kept their independence as they tried to unify with each other. Therefore, loyalty to the king was not strong.

Outside enemies, pagans within, and the ongoing threat of civil war are the three problems that shape the next part of our story.

Reflection

I keep the LORD always before me;
because he is at my right hand, I shall not be moved.
You show me the path of life.
In your presence there is fullness of joy;
in your right hand are pleasures forevermore.
(Psalm 16:8, 11)

What are your worries about the present? The future?

Should you turn to God more often as the psalmist does? When? Why?

PRAYER FOR TODAY

Here I Am, Lord

Side one: Here I am, Lord, yearning for your voice among many voices that tug, beckon, and entice me.

Side two: Here I am, Lord, straining to hear your whisper among the many whispers throughout the day.

Side one: Here I am, Lord, searching the stillness for signs of your presence and of your will for me.

Side two: I am ready, Lord. Speak, I am listening. May I know what it is you want for me. May I hear your word deep in my heart.

All: Lord, we try so hard to follow you, yet sometimes what we do is not what you want us to do. Help us continue to listen to your directions and to remember that even when we go astray, you are there, gently calling us back. Amen.

E. C.

HOMEWORK

very good

Covenant Puzzle

J e r i **C** h o

J **O** n a t h a n

D a **V** i d

J **E** R U S A L E M

N A T H A N

S **A** M U E L

S A M S O **N**

B a **T** h s h e b a

1. The walled city destroyed by Joshua is called Jericho.
2. Jonathan is the son of Saul.
3. David unified the twelve tribes.
4. David set up Jerusalem as both the religious and political capital of the kingdom.
5. Nathan was a prophet and an advisor to David.
6. The priest and prophet who appointed Saul as king was Samuel.
7. Samson was a great military leader noted for his physical strength.
8. The mother of Solomon was Bathsheba.

5

A Short-Lived Golden Age

"I have built you an exalted house, a place for you to dwell in forever." (1 Kings 8:13)

A Word to the Wise . . . small-group activity

Read Sirach 8. This passage provides an example of various wisdom sayings found in the Wisdom literature that began to develop during this period and is now found in our Old Testament. Now choose one of the categories listed below and write your own wisdom saying of advice to that person or group:

Young people who want to be popular

Young people interested in joining a gang

Young people experimenting with drugs or alcohol

Other: ______________________________

My wisdom saying about life and how to live it!

____

____

____

Share your wisdom saying with the others in your group.

Setting the scene

The time: 970–900 B.C.E.

The place: the kingdom of Israel, formerly known as Canaan

The plot: Solomon, building on the religious and political foundations of his father, King David, expands the rule of Israel to its neighbors and brings fame and prosperity to the kingdom. Most important, he builds the Temple, which his father instructed him to do. Immediately after Solomon's death, the ten northern tribes rebel against Solomon's son, select their own king, and set up their own kingdom. With this, tragically, the golden age ends (1 Kings 3–14, 2 Chronicles 1–14).

Who's who?

King Solomon, the son of David, overshadowed everyone during this period. He ruled from 970 to 931 B.C.E.

The other people to note during this period are:

Rehoboam—Solomon's son who succeeded him to the throne and ruled from 931 to 913 B.C.E.

Jeroboam—the first king of the ten northern tribes who rebelled against Rehoboam; ruled from 931 to 910 B.C.E.

Check It Out!

Solomon seems to have gathered a kind of zoo in Jerusalem. In 2 Chronicles chapter 9, we read that his ships would come from Tarshish, bringing him apes and baboons. Also, Solomon's palace complex in Jerusalem was huge. On the property were four thousand stalls for his horses and chariots.

The Team

In your opinion, which player would you rather have on your team—a player who uses his or her skill to obtain a victory, knowing that he or she is the best player and making sure he or she has the ball most of the time, or the player who tries to use the skills of all of the players at each of their best moments to ensure success for all? Which one are you?

Solomon the king

When Solomon became king, he inherited a united kingdom where all twelve tribes of Israel had accepted David's rule. When these tribes worked together under Solomon's kingship, they proved to be a strong military force. With their support, Solomon subdued many of the neighboring peoples and made important alliances with others (2 Chronicles 1:13–17).

During the brief period of Solomon's rule, Israel was not only safe from its enemies, but it also had their respect and, in some cases, their tribute of gold and other taxes. The ragged, wandering band of escaped slaves had become a nation to be reckoned with. This, as it turns out, was one of the high points of Israel's history in terms of being a worldly power. No wonder it became legendary, a kind of golden age the children of Abraham could only dream about in later days.

A Place of Honor

Solomon built a huge and expensive temple for the Ark of the Covenant. Draw and design a sacred place for your most prized possession.

The Temple

At the beginning of his reign, Solomon was a deeply religious person like his father. His faith and loyalty to God and the covenant were sincere and strong. He took very seriously his father's promise to build a temple. It was to be a place where the Ark of the Covenant would be permanently enshrined, where daily sacrifices could be offered, and where all Israel could gather to celebrate the great feasts. The Temple of Jerusalem took seven years to complete.

Because of Israel's new-found wealth and power, Solomon was able to build a fine temple. He gathered all the best materials: cedar, gold, silver, and precious stones, and he employed all the best artisans he could find (2 Chronicles 2–8).

Temple—a building where the Israelite people worshiped God
Church—a place where Christians gather to pray and to celebrate the sacraments

Check It Out

The plan of the Temple of Jerusalem built by Solomon was simply a larger, more permanent version of the tabernacle used by Moses to house the Ark of the Covenant. The Temple proper was actually a rather small building consisting of one room called the *Holy of Holies* where the Ark was kept and where God's presence was especially reverenced. A larger room called the *Holy Place* was where the altar of incense stood. Only the priests could enter these two rooms. The remainder of the Temple consisted of a porch or *court* and storerooms.

Solomon also built a magnificent palace for himself alongside the Temple. With both the Temple and the palace in Jerusalem, the city became a beautiful and bustling religious, political, commercial, and cultural center for the Israelites and for all surrounding peoples. These really were the glory days of Israel.

A model of ancient Jerusalem and the Temple of Solomon

Math Quiz

The standard measure used by the Israelites in building was a cubit, which was about eighteen inches. Solomon's Temple was 60 X 20 X 25 cubits. Figure out how big that was in feet.

Answer: length ___________ ft. width ___________ ft. height ___________ ft.

Solomon's House of the Forest of the Lebanon was 100 X 50 X 30 cubits. How big was that in feet?

Answer: length ___________ ft. width ___________ ft. height ___________ ft.

Solomon the man

As we said, Solomon was deeply religious. He was also gifted with extraordinary wisdom. Even today, some people use the expression "as wise as Solomon" to describe a wise person. Unfortunately, there was a flaw in Solomon's character. His fame, power, and wealth eventually went to his head and he became proud. The palace he built for himself surpassed the beauty of God's Temple (1 Kings 7).

Scripture Search

Read 1 Kings 3:16–28.

Why did Solomon's decision to cut the baby in two provide a solution to the argument? Children in today's world often feel like they have been split in two when their parents separate or divorce. If Solomon had to decide a child custody case today, would this same kind of tactic work?

Faithful, Rich, Famous, and Powerful— Is It possible?

Do you think it is possible to be rich, powerful, successful, and still be sincerely religious? Why or why not? Can you think of an example of someone who is rich and powerful and also religious?

To maintain himself in the kind of grandeur he desired, Solomon began to extract heavy taxes from the people and imposed forced labor on them to complete all his building projects. Solomon became something of a tyrant, like the kings of other nations. Toward the end of his reign, there were rumblings of rebellion among the people.

Greed!

Have you ever wanted something so badly that you were willing to steal, borrow, or beg to get it? If you didn't get what you wanted, wasn't that the worst feeling in the world? Looking back at events like this, can you believe that the desire you had to have what you wanted overcame you that strongly? Describe an event similar to this and the feelings you had. Try to put a description to the feeling and experience of greed.

____

____

____

____

____

There was another flaw in Solomon's character. His sexual appetites were often uncontrolled. According to 1 Kings, chapter 11, he eventually gathered a harem of 700 "royal wives" and 300 concubines! It was not considered immoral in those days for a man to have more than one wife, provided he could care for each of them and their children. So a king who was wealthy like Solomon could be expected to have more wives than an ordinary man. Yet, one thousand wives is a bit extreme by any standard.

For Solomon, the real problem wasn't the number of wives, it was that most of them were from foreign (that is, of a different religion) nations, a fact that aided him in making political alliances. Rather than force his wives to accept the covenant and worship his God, Solomon allowed them to continue to worship their gods. This occurred right in the shadow of the Temple.

Solomons of Today

Can you think of five famous people who do not live according to the values and example set by Jesus, yet their status in our society causes us to overlook their actions and still let them hold positions of influence or power?

____

____

____

____

____

Solomon's tolerance of the various religions of his wives became a scandal to the people, especially since it was his responsibility as king to be the religious leader and defender of the covenant. Despite God's warnings, Solomon continued to allow these practices. Eventually, God grew angry and turned against him.

CATECHISM CLIP

Christ is the true temple of God, "the place where his glory dwells"; by the grace of God, Christians also become temples of the Holy Spirit, living stones out of which the Church is built. (1197)

Scripture Search

God's chosen leader, Solomon, was tempted to worship other gods. He gave into these temptations and was punished by God. What theme often seen in the Hebrew Scriptures is repeated here? Can you name other stories in the Hebrew Scriptures where this theme is evidenced?

____

____

____

____

____

____

____

____

____

CATECHISM CLIP

Christ's call to conversion continues to resound in the lives of Christians. This second conversion *is an uninterrupted task for the whole Church who, "clasping sinners to her bosom, [is] at once holy and always in need of purification, [and] follows constantly the path of penance and renewal."* [LG 8§3.] . . . *(1428)*

A divided kingdom

Even before Solomon died, it was obvious that the reign would be taken away from Solomon's son. Through the prophet Ahijah, God called Jeroboam to mount a rebellion. Solomon tried to kill Jeroboam, but Jeroboam escaped to Egypt (1 Kings 11:26–40).

At Solomon's death, the people gathered to proclaim Rehoboam, Solomon's son, the new king. Jeroboam, hearing of Solomon's death, returned to claim the throne, but he was unsuccessful at the time. The elders advised Rehoboam that it was time for reform. They told him that if he wanted the ten rebellious northern tribes to remain loyal, he should treat them less harshly than his father had, easing up on taxes and so forth. Rehoboam rejected this advice and threatened to rule even more strictly than his father.

This was Jeroboam's cue to call the ten northern tribes to break from Rehoboam. They did. Rehoboam, of course, attempted to force the rebellious tribes back into obedience. They fought back, and Rehoboam failed. From this day forward, the twelve tribes of Israel were never united again. For the next two hundred years, there was almost constant fighting between the northern and southern kingdoms.

New names

The only tribe that remained loyal to the throne of David was the southern tribe of Judah. From then on, the southern kingdom is referred to in the Bible as *Judah* or the *Kingdom of Judah*. The ten northern tribes, on the other hand, become known in Scripture as the *Kingdom of Israel*.

Scripture Search

Small-group work

Read 2 Chronicles 1:1–13.

If you could ask God for just one thing with the assurance that God would grant your request, for what would you ask? Why would you request this? Would someone tell you it is impractical or impossible? Explain.

Compare your response with others in your group.

____

____

____

____

____

Bad times begin

Once the ten northern tribes broke off, Solo-mon's southern kingdom was reduced overnight to a mere shadow of its former size, power, and wealth. For the next two hundred years, it spent much of its energy fighting against the northern tribes. In doing this, it didn't have the might to protect itself from its foreign enemies as it had been able to do in the past.

The southern kingdom did have one thing going for it—the Temple. Most of the peoples of the northern tribes were still faithful to the God of Abraham, so they still looked to Jerusalem as the holy city where their God dwelled in the Temple, the center of their religious life. Jeroboam, the first king of the new, northern kingdom of Israel, realized that as long as this was the case, there was always a danger that his people would be lured back to allegiance to the kingdom of Judah.

Church Community

Some people say that the church is the center of the community, meaning that this is the group or boundaries by which they are known. Is this true with your church?

So Jeroboam established important religious centers among the northern tribes. He also established special feasts to compete with the pilgrimage feasts held at Jerusalem. In short, Jeroboam established parallel traditions to rival the traditional worship at Jerusalem. In time, the religious traditions of the northern kingdom could hardly be recognized as those the Israelites had brought with them to Canaan four hundred years earlier.

Two theologies

Remember how we said that the Old Testament first began as oral tradition, developed into written accounts, and finally, was edited and put together in the form we have today. Well, many of the first written accounts have their origin around this time.

While the Israelites were enslaved in Egypt and wandering in the desert, there wasn't much time for reflecting, writing, and keeping records. Once things settled down and a cultural life developed around the time of the court of David and Solomon, people were assigned to keep records. It is these records that later become parts of the Bible.

Much of the oral tradition of the covenant and the Law of Moses was put in more formal writing during this time, too. But with the split into northern and southern kingdoms, the scholars and priests who did most of this kind of writing were in two different places—the northern court and the southern court. As a result, each group reflected on Israel's history from a different point of view. The North, cut off from the Temple and from the throne of David, focused on the covenant and on fidelity to the Law of Moses. In the South, the focus shifted to the covenant God made with David when he promised to preserve David's throne and send a messiah who would restore the kingdom to its former glory.

It's Your Opinion

Interview two people separately at different times about a popular movie they saw and what they thought of it. Do they share the same opinions or does their own view of things create a difference in opinion? Have you had an experience where your view on something was entirely different than another person's? How do you usually resolve this difference?

Wisdom literature

The Bible's Wisdom literature started being written during the time of Solomon. Much of the Wisdom literature found in the Old Testament is not in the Hebrew Scriptures. The basis for the Books of Proverbs, Ecclesiastes, and the Song of Songs can be traced to this period. If they weren't written by Solomon, they do reflect his influence on the thinking of Israel. It was also during this time that many of the psalms were collected. The other books that make up the Wisdom literature—Job and Wisdom—were written much later.

The Wisdom literature adds some new insights into Israel's unique covenant relationship with God. It also explores themes common to all humanity. Some of these themes are profound, such as the question of evil and suffering explored in the Book of Job. Some of the themes deal with everyday life, such as choosing good friends or being a good parent, all of which can be found in the Book of Proverbs.

Scripture Search

Read Job 29:1–10 and 30:1–10. Has there ever been a time when you felt that you wanted to return to a time in your life when things seemed to be going better? Describe this experience. How did you get yourself out of this misery? In the Book of Job, God finally tells Job that God has the answers to all the questions and it is not for humankind to know everything that God knows (chapters 38–42). Does God's answer to Job's misery help you accept yours?

Lessons to be learned

During this period, the lesson to be learned is the same old one that God has been repeating over and over since he first called Abraham: Israel's peace and happiness come from fidelity to their God and the covenant. Trusting in wealth, power, or the gods of their neighbors guarantees disaster.

Wrap-Up

The reigns of David and Solomon were the glory days of the children of Abraham. Though this glory didn't last long, it makes a lasting impression on all future generations. These years become the standard by which all future periods are judged. They become the "ideal" the children of Abraham hoped and prayed would one day be restored when the promised messiah came.

Under this veneer of glory, the age-old weaknesses of the children of Abraham remained and eventually lead to their decline. The twelve tribes had a hard time getting along together. The people were all too easily lured away from the covenant and into other religious practices. Solomon, who should have been the religious leader and defender of the people, became the victim of his own success and turned into a proud tyrant. Even the Temple, which Solomon built in his days of religious fervor, was overshadowed by the grandeur of the palace he built for himself.

So by 900 B.C.E., the once grand kingdom of David and Solomon was split in two and the decline of both kingdoms began. By 587 B.C.E., both kingdoms have completely disappeared, along with Solomon's Temple. We'll tell the story of that decline in the next chapter.

Honoring God—Sometimes!

Do you think people your age have a respect for their church building? Is it appreciated for the gift of God's presence seen there in the Blessed Sacrament? Why or why not? What could young people do to witness to their reverence for the church and the Blessed Sacrament?

____
____
____
____
____
____

Check It Out

At one time, the mountainsides of Lebanon were covered with giant cedars, noted for their fragrance and resistance to decay. Solomon floated large barges of these cedars down the coast and then carried them inland to be used in building the Temple and his palace. The Scriptures often make reference to the famed cedars of Lebanon.

Reflection

[Solomon] said, "O LORD, God of Israel, there is no God like you,
in heaven or on earth, keeping covenant in steadfast love with your servants
who walk before you with all their heart . . .
(2 Chronicles 6:14)

Name some ways God shows his kindness to you.

Are these ways obvious or are they hidden gifts that you believe only come from God rather than luck? Explain.

Overlooking the Plain of Jezreel

PRAYER FOR TODAY

Pause for a few moments to be quiet and to become aware of God's presence. Then pray together Psalm 25:1–14.

Side one: To you, O LORD, I lift up my soul. O my God, in you I trust; do not let me be put to shame; do not let my enemies exult over me.

Side two: Do not let those who wait for you be put to shame; let them be ashamed who are wantonly treacherous. Make me to know your ways, O LORD; teach me your paths. Lead me in your truth, and teach me, for you are the God of my salvation; for you I wait all day long.

Side one: Be mindful of your mercy, O LORD, and of your steadfast love, for they have been from of old. Do not remember the sins of my youth or my transgressions, according to your steadfast love remember me, for your goodness' sake, O LORD!

Side two: Good and upright is the LORD; therefore he instructs sinners in the way. He leads the humble in what is right, and teaches the humble his way.

Side one: All the paths of the LORD are steadfast love and faithfulness, for those who keep his covenant and his decrees. For your name's sake, O LORD, pardon my guilt, for it is great.

Side two: Who are they that fear the LORD? He will teach them the way that they should choose. They will abide in prosperity, and their children shall possess the land. The friendship of the LORD is for those who fear him, and he makes his covenant known to them.

All: Loving God, may I ever keep my thoughts focused on you and your kindness. In the midst of all my busyness and unhappiness, remind me that you are always near. Be my guide, my protector, my advisor, my friend. I ask this in the name of your Son, Jesus, our Risen Savior. Amen.

HOMEWORK

Fill in the Blanks

1. Judah was the only southern tribe to remain loyal to the throne of David.
2. The one thing going for the southern tribes was the temple.
3. Questions of evil and suffering are explored in the Book of Job.
4. The reign of Solomon is considered the Golden Age.
5. God called the prophet Ahijah to tell Jeroboam to mount a rebellion against Solomon.
6. Chronicles is the book of the Bible that describes in detail what was involved in building the temple.
7. The northern tribes are referred to in the Bible as the Kingdom of Israel.
8. To maintain his grand style of living, Solomon extracted heavy taxes from the people.
9. Solomon built a temple in Jerusalem.
10. Toward the end of Solomon's reign, there were rumblings of rebellion among the people.
11. Jeroboam became the first king of the ten northern tribes.
12. Jeroboam escaped his death by fleeing to Egypt.
13. Most of Solomon's wives were from foreign nations.
14. Rehoboam was Solomon's son who succeeded him as king.
15. God gifted Solomon with wisdom.

Ahijah	Israel	rebellion
Chronicles	Jeroboam	Rehoboam
Egypt	Jerusalem	taxes
foreign	Job	temple
Golden Age	Judah	wisdom

6

Prophets, Kings, and Conquerors

Therefore thus says the Lord GOD: An adversary shall surround the land, and strip you of your defense; and your strongholds shall be plundered. (Amos 3:11)

God Says to You . . .

Prophets are sent by God to speak in God's name to warn, instruct, and console the people. If God sent a prophet today, what words would God have the prophet speak in each of the following situations?

1. A word of warning to society

____

____

2 A word of advice to the Church

____

____

3. A word of consolation to the poor and oppressed

____

____

Compare your responses with those of the others in your group.

Setting the scene

The time: 900 B.C.E. to 587 B.C.E.

The place: the northern kingdom of Israel, the southern kingdom of Judah, Assyria, and Babylon

The plot: The northern and southern kingdoms go through a long decline, both religiously and politically. Great prophets warn of coming destruction and try to call the people back to fidelity to their God. Although there are a few attempts at reform, the decline continues until both kingdoms are finally destroyed by outside invaders. By 587 B.C.E., Jerusalem and the Temple are leveled. Only the poor and some foreigners live in the land promised to Abraham.

Who's who?

This period of Israel's history was dominated by the great prophets whom Yahweh called forth to proclaim God's word to the people. Some were sent to the northern kingdom of Israel and some preach to the kingdom of Judah in the south.

Those sent to the northern kingdom included:

Elijah and Elisha—the first two great prophets of the period who preached between 870 and 840 B.C.E.

Amos—the shepherd prophet from Tekoa who preached around 750 B.C.E.

Hosea—the prophet of the covenant who preached around 730 B.C.E., just before the northern kingdom was conquered by the Assyrian king Sargon II

The prophets sent to the southern kingdom included:

Isaiah—perhaps one of the best known prophets because so much of his preaching has been preserved; preached around 740–700 B.C.E.

Micah—preached about the same time as Isaiah but was not quite as well known

Jeremiah—his preaching began around 627 B.C.E., just before the destruction of the southern kingdom, and continued throughout that ordeal until around 587 B.C.E.

Ezekiel—among the first group of captives carried off to Babylon around 598 B.C.E.; preached among the captives to keep their hope alive during their captivity

Decline and fall of the two kingdoms

Although Solomon ruled supreme in Israel and the surrounding territories, his actual control over neighboring nations was never strong. What control he had was gained more by treaties and alliances than by actual force. So when his kingdom was divided in 922 B.C.E., the two smaller kingdoms became fair game once more for ambitious neighboring nations. The two kingdoms were able to hold their own against other small nations, but proved to be no match for the new "superpowers" that emerged between 800 and 600 B.C.E.

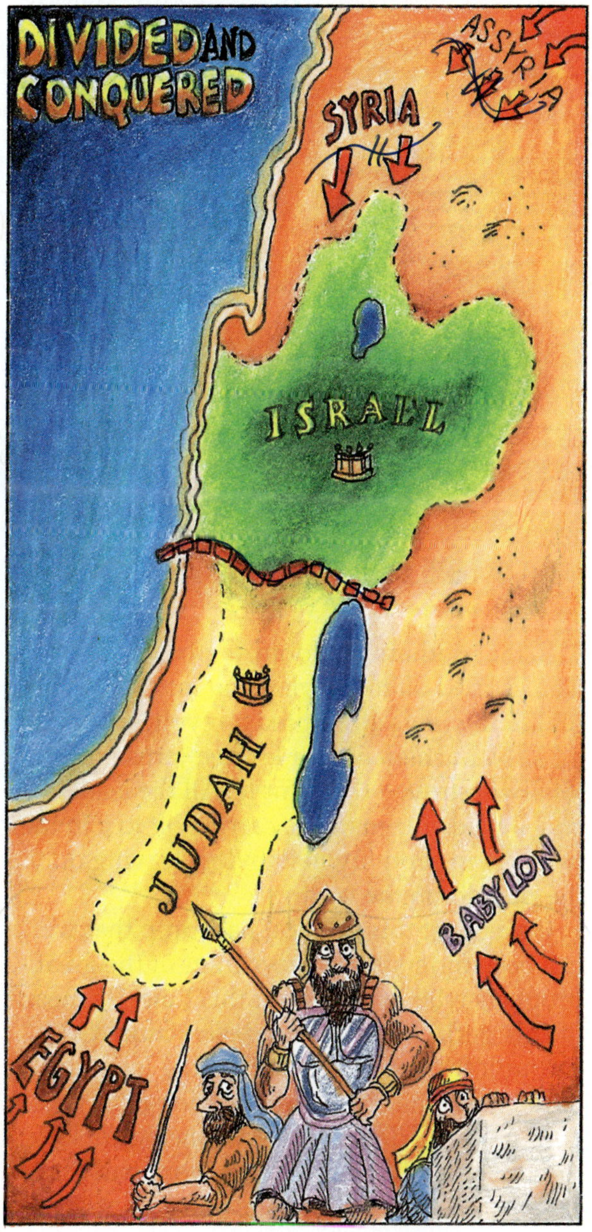

In the northern kingdom, the survivors were carried off into slavery and never heard from again. These ten northern tribes disappeared from history and now are often referred to as the *ten lost tribes of Israel*.

What Did You Say???

In a small group, develop a coded language to which only your group will know the code. Send a message to another group using your code. If the other group can't break the code after a certain length of time, give them your code to use in translating your message. Have them send an answer back to you. How long does this conversational exchange take compared to what it would take if you both were speaking the same language?

____
____
____
____
____
____

Cultural Shock

A group of people from another country has captured you and brought you to their faraway country. You are now a slave in a country where the language, culture, and laws are different and frightening. How would you take care of yourself?

In the southern kingdom, a group of hostages were carried off to Babylon and into slavery. The remaining Jews attempted a revolt, so in 587 B.C.E., Nebuchadenezzar leveled Jerusalem and totally destroyed the Temple. All the leaders and skilled citizens were carried off to join their relatives in captivity in Babylon, leaving only the poorest on the land.

It's against this political backdrop that we can best understand the writings of the great prophets who lived during this time. By means of this period of political destruction, God, through the prophets, helped the Israelites understand the true nature of their faith within their personal despair. Despite their great losses, they became a stronger and more trusting people who knew that their covenant with God would not be in vain.

Catechism Clip

Through the prophets, God forms his people in the hope of salvation, in the expectation of a new and everlasting Covenant intended for all, to be written on their hearts. [Cf. Isa *2:2–4;* Jer *31:31–34;* Heb *10:16.] . . . (64)*

A Prophet Today

Make a list of some modern-day prophets that have an impact on you. (Don't forget that a prophet speaks publicly about God and faith to others.) How do you see the people on your list fulfilling the definition of a prophet?

____
____
____
____
____

Kings and corruption

The kingdoms needed purifying. Although it was outside powers who actually destroyed the two kingdoms, the real problems weren't external. The prophets made it clear that these foreign powers were simply instruments God used to punish the unfaithful people. It was their own internal flaws that lead to their downfall.

Trouble Within

Think about a time when a member or members of your family seemed confused, hurt, or uneasy. What caused the confusion, hurt feelings, and disruption? Did the cause come from within or outside the family unit?

The people committed two different sins. First, they violated the most basic religious principle of their covenant with God. Rather than trusting in God completely, they continually worshiped other gods along with the God of Abraham. In addition, they often relied on treaties and alliances with other nations to help them against their enemies, rather than relying on God's power to defend them, as they had in the days of Joshua. Even when the people did worship the God of Abraham, it was often just empty ritual, not sincere worship from the heart (Isaiah 1:11–16).

Second, they violated the other basic principle of the covenant—treating one another with justice. An upper class developed in both the northern and southern kingdoms. This noble class became wealthy and powerful and began to live in self-indulgent luxury while ignoring the needs of the poor, the widows, and the orphans in their midst. Even worse, it often cheated these people and treated them like slaves (Amos 5:7–13).

CATECHISM CLIP

"On Sundays and other holy days of obligation the faithful are bound . . . to abstain from those labors and business concerns which impede the worship to be rendered to God, the joy which is proper to the Lord's Day, or the proper relaxation of mind and body" (CIC, can. 1247). (2193)

Cafeteria Catholics

Some people accuse American Catholics of picking and choosing what they want to believe and follow from their religion, much like choosing food from a cafeteria line. What do you think? Do you tend to follow the parts of your religion that you like and ignore those parts that you don't like?

CATECHISM CLIP

"Sunday . . . is to be observed as the foremost holy day of obligation in the universal Church (CIC, can. 1246§1). "On Sundays and other holy days of obligation the faithful are bound to participate in the Mass" (CIC, can. 1247). (2192)

The prophets

Prophets were persons called by God (sometimes in dramatic fashion—read Isaiah 6:1–8) to speak in the name of God to the king and the people. As proof that they were truly God's messengers, their preaching was sometimes accompanied by signs or miracles (1 Kings 17:17–24).

In general, those chosen as prophets felt unqualified and weren't eager to accept the mission. In most cases, the message they brought was not very pleasant. It predicted bad times and called the people to turn from their infidelity, injustice, and self-indulgence. As a result, the prophets were usually persecuted and sometimes killed. Being a prophet was and still is a high-risk vocation.

Check It Out

Poor Jeremiah had a very rough time. Once, for example, his enemies beat him and then put him in stocks (Jeremiah 20:1–4). Another time they put him in a cistern where he sank into its muddy floor (Jeremiah 38:4–6).

Check It Out

Prophets are not just a part of the Hebrew tradition. In the Islam religion, Muslims consider Muhammad to be the last of the prophets. Mormons consider their founder, Joseph Smith, to be a prophet in keeping with the Hebrew Scriptures tradition.

Bad News

Have you ever had a message delivered to you that you did not want to hear? For example, you had to babysit your younger brothers and sisters rather than go to your friend's house because your parents were working late. Did you express your anger toward the messenger instead of at the message?

Besides this general message of repentance-or-else, the prophets also called the people to a new, deeper understanding of God and their covenant relationship with God. Intermingled with the prophets "doom and gloom" messages, you will find wonderful passages of hope, marvelous insights into the depth of God's love, gentleness, and mercy, as well as soaring visions of God's power and majesty. Also, God's promise to David to send a messiah takes on a new, deeper meaning through the prophets, especially through Isaiah.

Who were the prophets?

With their unique personalities, the prophets were quite distinct from one another. You'll find their personalities affected their messages and the way they delivered their messages. Also, each prophet was preaching at a particular time to either the people in the northern or southern kingdom. The political situation of that time, the king who was ruling, the kinds of infidelities that the people were committing—all these gave each prophet's message a certain concrete quality. They refered to specific places, specific kings and nations, and specific behaviors of the ruling king or the people.

These are the prophets!

Amos was an uneducated shepherd who warned the northern kingdom that Assyria will conquer them.

Isaiah was an educated noble who spoke with a poetic quality and predicted the fall of Judah after the northern kingdom fell.

Hosea was married to a religious prostitute and used his experience as a symbol for Israel's unfaithful relationship with God.

Jeremiah sometimes acted out his message in dramatic fashion. He predicted the capture of Jerusalem and the destruction of the Temple by Nebuchadenezzar.

Ezekiel was a seer given to ecstatic visions and also sometimes acted out his message.

Elijah was a mystery man who appeared on the scene like the wind and disappeared in the same way.

Micah, like Amos, was a simple peasant.

To understand each prophet and their message, you need to have a general idea of the personality of the prophet and the situation within which each was preaching.

Talk to Me

You have been asked to share (with the people listed below) your science project of growing mold on bread. How will you address each crowd, how detailed will your presentation be, and how will you dress? Does the presentation need to be different with each group? Why?

- A group of science professors
- A group of your peers
- A first grade class

Scripture Search

Small-group activity

Read the following passages that give examples of how prophets sometimes acted out their message: Jeremiah 13:1–14 and Ezekiel 4:1–17. If a prophet today wanted to speak out against one of the following practices, what would be an action the prophet could use to dramatize the message? Choose one and then suggest an action.

- Treating people who are poor unjustly
- Insincere religious practices
- Putting trust in riches rather than in God

Compare your work with the others in your group.

Check It Out

For Christians, John the Baptizer, who announced the coming of Jesus as the Messiah, is considered to be, in a unique sense, the last of the prophets.

Timeless message

While it's true that each prophet spoke at a particular time to a particular situation, the message of these prophets also has a timeless quality. Amos's call for social justice is as valid today as it was when he preached in the courts of the kingdom of Israel in 750 B.C.E. (Amos 5:7–12). Isaiah's descriptions of the suffering servant that God would send to redeem the people continue to help us grasp the depth of Jesus' love for us (Isaiah 53). Ezekiel helps us grasp the idea of our own personal responsibility to remain faithful to God (Ezekiel 33:10–20). Hosea helps us grasp the tender love God feels toward each of us and for the Church as a whole (Hosea 11:1–4).

Prophet Wanted!

With all of the advances in technology and as we move closer toward playing God, why do we need a prophet for today? Explain and give examples.

The prophetic tradition

The role all true prophets had in common was that they were spokespersons or messengers for God. Another common thread was that it was God who took the initiative and entered into a special relationship with each prophet. Think about it: becoming a prophet wasn't the kind of career you chose as a youth and then went to school to learn how to do. In fact, as we said earlier, most prophets weren't too happy being called by God.

Not Me, Lord!

Read the following passages. What response did each prophet give when called by the Lord?

- Exodus 4:10–17 ______________________________
- Jeremiah 1:1–6 ______________________________
- Ezekiel 1:28–2:1–7 ______________________________
- Jonah 1:1–17 ______________________________

You, a Prophet!

What would you do if God asked you to be a prophet and speak a life-saving message to your community? Would you challenge God or accept the position, despite your fears?

Check It Out

To listen to a prophet took a certain openness and willingness to listen to the message rather than focus on the messenger. That so many prophets were ignored, persecuted, or martyred tells us a great deal about the attitude of the people to whom they preached. These people simply didn't want to hear the truth because it would mean admitting their sin. It would mean giving up their selfish living or the control they had over the poor and weak.

We can't really know how God told the prophets what to say. The Scriptures often refer to visions and dreams, or simply have God "dictating" the message to the prophet. This much we do know: the prophets were deeply spiritual people. They held their God at the center of their lives and spent much time in prayer and reflection. Whether they received God's message dramatically in special visions and dreams, or whether it came to them in the more ordinary process of their prayerful reflection, it really doesn't matter. They no longer were speaking for themselves or giving their own ideas. The true nature of their relationship with God was seen as they addressed the people and proclaimed what God had taught them to say.

Check It Out

The complete listing of the prophets in the Old Testament includes the following: Isaiah, Jeremiah, Ezekiel, Daniel, Baruch, Hosea, Joel, Amos, Obadiah, Jonah, Micah, Nahum, Habakkuk, Zephaniah, Haggai, Zechariah, and Malachi.

I Spy a Prophet

Look around the classroom and imagine one of your peers or imagine one of your family members as an important leader of a group of people. What qualities do you see in that person that makes him or her a candidate for this role? Be sure to share your answer with the person you chose.

And more than a prophet . . .

If you look at who a prophet is (a person chosen by God and then instructed by God to give his message to the people), you realize there were many prophets who also carried out other leadership roles at the same time. Moses was clearly a prophet, perhaps the greatest in the Old Testament. Samuel, the judge, was a prophet. David was a prophet, for the psalms he wrote have a prophetic quality. Elijah and Elisha are two famous prophets, even if their teachings aren't contained in special books. Miriam and Deborah are women prophets also mentioned in Scripture. Some prophets are only referred to in Scripture as "a prophet said."

Women as Leaders

The Bible has left out of its main text many stories of women because of the culture of the times and the belief that women were not equal to men. Name the women who have played an important role in your faith development and how they affected you.

This much is clear: rather than appearing directly to the people, God seemed to prefer to teach by using ordinary messengers like you. In hindsight, people like Moses don't seem so ordinary, especially since he spoke with God. But when he first appeared on the scene in Egypt and told the enslaved Hebrews that he was sent by God to deliver them, Moses was just another Hebrew with ordinary human characteristics. For example, God did not let Moses' stuttering get in the way of leading God's people.

Amos was about as ordinary as you get. He was an uneducated shepherd from the southern kingdom. You can imagine what the people thought when they first saw him dressed in a shepherd's rags and speaking with an accent. Yet he dared to speak in the courts of the northern kingdom of Israel and began to tell the king and rich nobles what was wrong with them.

Scripture Search

Read Jeremiah 9:1–21.

Is our society in danger of being destroyed because of its own sinfulness? Why or why not? Can you think of one example of environmental damage and one example of political damage that is caused by sin and may destroy our planet?

Key faith lessons

It seems the people to whom the prophets first preached seldom actually learned from them. Although there were a few attempts at reform from time to time, the kings and people for the most part continued in their life of infidelity, injustice, and self-indulgence right to the end.

It was only after the destruction of Judah, while the people were captive in Babylon, that the teachings of the prophets finally began to sink in. As we'll see in the next chapter, the real religious reform began during captivity and ended after the surviving people were allowed to return to Judah.

The messages of the prophets have endured throughout the centuries and have timeless value. You can read and reread the prophets and continue to discover new insights into who God really is, what fidelity to God really means, and what it means to treat one another justly. We can also continually gain new insights into the person and mission of the promised messiah as we read the prophets.

Wrap-Up

Despite the warnings from the prophets, the people continued a life of infidelity and injustice. In the end, their sinfulness led to the destruction of both the northern and southern kingdoms. The ten tribes of the northern kingdom disappeared altogether and the people of Judah were carried off to Babylon.

Although the messages of the prophets were largely ignored when first preached, the faith of the children of Abraham was maturing and was quickly becoming the foundation on which our own faith would be established.

Reflection

Then I heard the voice of the Lord saying, "Whom shall I send, and who will go for us?"
And I said, "Here I am; send me!"
(Isaiah 6:8)

What kind of work do you feel the Lord is calling you to do?

What would be your reasons for rejecting this invitation?

PRAYER FOR TODAY

Leader: Lord Jesus, you have chosen each of us to spread your word. We now place ourselves in your hands and pledge ourselves to you.

Side one: To be chosen by you is a privilege; we will need your strength to do your will.

Side two: To be called to do your work, Lord, is to be sent forth; we will need your courage to complete your work.

Side one: To be chosen by you is to know we are loved; we will need your steadfast heart to share that love with one another.

Side two: Sharing your word, Lord, will lead us to a deeper faith in you; help us share in love and joy.

All: Loving God, help us follow and live the words of the prophet Micah, who told the people what the Lord required—"to act justly, to love kindly, and to walk humbly with our God." Amen.

Extra Credit HOMEWORK

Read the following passages. Then decide what meaning each passage might have for us today.

Isaiah 5:8–10

Meaning today:

Isaiah 5:11–13

Meaning today:

Ezekiel 33:14–17

Meaning today:

Amos 8:4–6

Meaning today:

Micah 3:5

Meaning today:

7

A Nation Rebuilds

"I will let you find me, says the LORD, and I will restore your fortunes and gather you from all the nations and all the places where I have driven you, says the LORD, and I will bring you back to the place from which I sent you into exile." (Jeremiah 29:14)

Feet of Clay—small-group activity

The popular expression *feet of clay* is rooted in a story found in the Book of Daniel, chapter 2, when he interpreted the king's dream of a huge statue that was destroyed by a stone because it rested on feet of clay. Take a minute to read the passage.

A strong foundation is important for what is to be built on top of it. How can you build a strong foundation for each of the following areas of your life? What could happen if the foundation has "feet of clay"?

Your education

____

Your friendships

____

Your faith

____

Compare your answers with the others in your group.

Setting the scene

The time: 587–333 B.C.E.

The place: Babylon (modern-day Iraq) and Judea

The plot: Jerusalem is in ruins and the children of Abraham are once again in exile in a foreign land. They remain in exile for fifty years. Then, in a sudden reversal of fortunes, in 538 B.C.E. they are freed to return home to rebuild their kingdom and their faith. The religious reform is successful, but the rebuilding of their kingdom doesn't go as well.

Check It Out

Ancient Babylonia, the seat of the Babylonian Empire, was situated between the Tigris and Euphrates Rivers. In its day, its capital, Babylon, was the greatest city that had ever been built. The wall around Babylon was eleven miles long. It boasted over 280 temples and altars in worship of its gods and goddesses.

Who's who

Ezekiel—the great prophet who kept the hope of the people alive during their exile and deepened their understanding of their covenant with God

Daniel—another great prophet who taught the people how to remain faithful during their exile

Cyrus I—king of the Persians who conquered Babylon in 538 B.C.E. and granted permission for the children of Abraham to return to Judea

Ezra—the religious leader who was sometimes called the "second Moses"; led the religious reform of the people between 450 and 425 B.C.E.

Nehemiah—the political leader of Judea who worked with Ezra to rebuild Judea

Haggai, Zechariah, Malachi, Obadiah, Joel, and Jonah—prophets who preached during this period of restoration

False Security

Have you ever had an experience where you didn't pay attention to the warning signs of trouble and you ended up with a problem? (Some examples: not doing the dishes despite your frustrated father's repeated warnings or feeling a cold coming on and staying out in the rain.) Identify three possible other warning signs. What are the results of ignoring these warning signs?

____

____

____

____

____

____

____

____

____

Learning the hard way

The people of Judah made a major mistake. They believed that they would always be safe. They believed that the God of gods had made them the chosen people and promised to protect them. God even dwelt in their midst in the Temple at Jerusalem. Even at the last minute, God would always rescue them and drive the invaders back as he had done so many times before.

Lulled by this false security, the people tended to ignore all the prophets that God sent to warn them about the covenant being a two-way relationship. Again and again, the prophets told the people that they couldn't totally ignore their own responsibilities to be faithful and yet still expect God to protect them.

There Was a Man . . .

. . . who was in a terrible flood. He went to the roof of his house and prayed to God to save him. Just then a woman in a boat came by to rescue him, but the man declined, stating, "I asked God to save me and I will wait for him!" The water continued to climb to the point where the man was perched, and he continued to pray for God to save him. A helicopter flew by to rescue him, but the man declined, stating, "I asked God to save me and I will wait for him!" Now the man was getting very anxious and frantically prayed to God to save him. But alas, the water was too great and he eventually drowned. The man, upon meeting God in heaven, asked him, "Why did you not answer my prayers?" God replied, "I did! Where do you think the boat and the helicopter came from?"

Can you remember a time when you felt God answered your prayers but in a way different than you expected?

____

____

____

____

____

With Jerusalem and the Temple in ruins and the chosen people enslaved in Babylon, the message of the prophets finally began to sink in. The people began to realize that the real cause of all their trouble was their own infidelity. If only they had trusted in God. If only they had listened to the prophets, repented, and treated each other more justly, none of this would have happened.

Red Light

Have you ever been warned not to do something, but you chose to do it anyway? What were the consequences of not listening to the warning?

All was not lost

Although all seemed lost, a few embers of hope were still aglow.

One beacon of hope was the prophet Ezekiel. He was one of the first captives to be carried off to Babylon in 598 B.C.E., so when the rest of the captives arrived in 587 B.C.E., he was there to greet them. He assured them that all was not lost and that God had not abandoned them completely. If they repented, they would once again dwell in Judah.

It was this kind of teaching that kept hope alive and helped the captives recall the preaching of the other prophets, such as Isaiah, Jeremiah, Amos, and Hosea. They remembered that these prophets also promised that God would rescue the people and restore them in their own land. This period of exile became a period of renewing, purifying, and deepening of faith for the people.

Hope-Builders

Some people can take what seems like a tragedy and turn it into something positive. For example, an older couple owned a home with a yard between the bus stop and the local high school. Children were constantly cutting across the yard, using it as a shortcut between the two places. The couple eventually created a walking path and planted flowers along the path. They placed a bench near the path where they could sit and greet the children. They came to know many of the children by name, and some students would stop for a few minutes to visit with the couple before hurrying on their way.

Some people in our lives are perpetual hope-builders. They always speak positively, turning bad into good. Think of one person in your life who is like this and identify what effect they have on you.

____

____

____

____

____

____

____

____

Check It Out

Around 450 B.C.E., when Judah was trying to rebuild amid the rubble of Jerusalem, Greece entered into its great golden age. It was the age of such great artisans as Pericles and Plato.

Tested by fire

It would have been easy for the people of Judah to settle in Babylon, adopt the religion and customs of their captors, and begin a new life. To their credit, they didn't do that. In this land of exile, they began to follow the covenant more strictly than they had done in their own land. This change of heart is reflected in the Book of Daniel. It's a sad fact, but it sometimes takes great tragedies to force people to recognize their errors and to get their values straight.

Habits Are Hard to Break

What habit do you have that drives other people crazy? What would it take for you to change or to give up this habit? Sometimes even when people know their life may depend on changing, they still choose not to change. Why do you think this is?

CATECHISM CLIP

"The Church . . . will receive its perfection only in the glory of heaven," [LG 48.] at the time of Christ's glorious return. Until that day, "the Church progresses on her pilgrimage amidst this world's persecutions and God's consolations." [St. Augustine, De civ.Dei, *18, 51: PL 41, 614; cf. LG 8.] Here below she knows that she is in exile far from the Lord, and longs for the full coming of the Kingdom, when she will "be united in glory with her king." [LG 5; cf. 6; 2 Cor 5:6.]*

We were like people dreaming

Just as God had used foreign kings to punish the children of Abraham, God now used a foreign king to rescue his people. Ironically, the people were given plenty of warnings that they would be conquered and enslaved, yet they virtually had no warning that their rescue would come so suddenly. According to Psalm 126, it was a complete and joyful surprise. Verses one and two say it all: "When the LORD restored the fortunes of Zion, we were like those who dream. Then our mouth was filled with laughter, and our tongue with shouts of joy."

Shouts of Joy

Read Psalm 126. As the chosen people experienced their release from captivity, they could not contain themselves and praised the Lord with shouts of joy. Our faith tradition has many such songs. Look through your parish's song books to see if you can find other songs of praise or jubilation. List the songs' titles below. Is there a song on the top forty chart of today's popular music that is a song of joy, praise, or freedom? If possible, play the song for your class.

The political events securing this freedom were as follows: A new superpower, Persia, appeared on the scene around 600 B.C.E. By 538 B.C.E., the king of Persia, Cyrus I, conquered Babylon. Almost immediately, he decided to free the Jews and help them reestablish themselves in Judah (Ezra 1:1–11). We can't be sure what Cyrus' motives were for releasing the Jews. But for the Jews, it was clear that God was behind the decision.

Check It Out

Synagogues were first established by the Jews while they were captives in Babylon. Having no temple, they gathered in homes to pray and to support one another in faith. When Judah was rebuilt, just about every town outside Jerusalem established a synagogue where the people gathered on the Sabbath to hear the Scriptures and to pray.

Check it Out

After the return from exile, the chosen people began being referred to as the *Jewish people*, which was shortened to *Jews*.

The news of the release spread quickly to the exiles scattered throughout Babylon. A group assembled and prepared to return. Their former captors gave them supplies to help them get started. Even the king came forth and gave them some of the Temple furnishings Nebuchadenezzar had carried off.

Rebuilding

Imagine that an important building, like a school, a church, or a library, burned down. Make a list of five priorities that would have to be taken care of immediately after the fire. Rank them in the order of importance.

1. ______________________________
2. ______________________________
3. ______________________________
4. ______________________________
5. ______________________________

When you are finished, take a close look at your list. Did you put people's needs above the physical building, or did you do the opposite?

No welcome mat waiting

When this first wave of exiles returned, their joy quickly turned to sadness. Their elders had told them stories of Jerusalem as a proud, beautiful city with its glorious Temple, its gleaming palaces, its bustling market, but what they found when they returned was a ghost town filled with rubble and stray dogs. Instead of crowds lining the streets to welcome them back, they found a hostile people in neighboring Samaria ready to do whatever it took to keep the exiles from rebuilding Jerusalem.

The exiles were ready to work. Their first priority was to rebuild the Temple. So they began to plant crops for their food and their offerings to God.

Samaria attacked so often that the Jews found themselves working with a trowel in one hand and a spear in the other. Most of the crops failed. The people became discouraged, but prophets, such as Haggai and Zechariah, kept their hope alive.

Frustration!

A House of Cards—small-group activity

With your small group, take a deck of cards and try to build a house of cards. After two minutes of house-building, one person from each group should go visit another group's house. Without physically touching the house, the visiting person has ten seconds to try to knock down the group's house.

How frustrating was the house-building? Did you ever feel like giving up? Did members of your own group ever knock down your house? Did your group try to protect your house in any way? Was there a "prophet" in your group who kept offering encouragement and affirmation?

____

____

____

____

____

In time, new waves of exiles joined the group. With these reinforcements, they were better able to protect themselves and the rebuilding was more successful. By 520 B.C.E., a new Temple stood on the ruins of Solomon's Temple. It was not as large nor as well decorated, but it was their Temple. Now, their God dwelt in their midst once more.

Ezra and Nehemiah

Ezra became the religious leader of the people during this time. Under his guidance, official Temple worship was reestablished. The old religious feasts were celebrated once again. Just as important, Ezra reestablished the covenant and its laws as the guide for both the public and private lives of the people.

Nehemiah worked closely with Ezra. He had influence in the court of Persia and was able to get supplies and military help. Nehemiah is best known for organizing the Jews politically. He formed a citizen army and helped them fight off their neighboring enemies. Under his leadership, they were able to complete the rebuilding of the walls of Jerusalem and the city itself. By around 450 B.C.E., all of the former exiles were "back home."

Proceed with Caution

For many of us, when we are hurt one time doing something, we are more careful the next time we attempt it. This caution occurs for almost anything, from touching a hot object to trusting a friend again. Make a list of five experiences from your own life in which you proceeded with more caution the second time than the first.

____

____

____

____

____

Nature of religious reform

Remembering that all their past problems stemmed from being unfaithful to the covenant, the Jews made obedience to the covenant the centerpiece of their lives. At times, their concern for the covenant tended toward a kind of legalism, where the laws governed every detail of their lives, from how often they should wash their hands to how far they could walk on the Sabbath.

This fear also caused the Jews to remember that much of their past infidelity to the covenant stemmed from the bad influence of their neighbors. Many of the Jews began to try to cut themselves off from all unnecessary association with other groups. Certain acts, such as marriage to non-Jews, were strictly forbidden (Ezra 9). Even brushing up against a non-Jew eventually was seen as making a devout Jew "unclean" and required special purifying rituals.

This kind of religious legalism continued to grow among some people until the time of Jesus. By then, it actually became an obstacle for many to be faithful to the true spirit of the covenant. Just think, legalism started out in the time of Ezra as a sincere effort by the people to reform and be faithful to the covenant as the prophets had told them, and it became the one thing that blocked some of the Jews from believing in Jesus.

Scripture Search

Read Nehemiah 8:1–6.

1. How do we show our respect for the word of God today?

2. List three new understandings of your faith or faith traditions that you have gained since starting this course.

Your Sacred Books

Make a list of three of your all-time favorite books. What is it about these books that makes them special? Are there any similarities between the books you chose?

The sacred books

Another part of the people's religious reform was to begin to really appreciate the value of their religious writings, which had been developing over the centuries. The main focus, of course, was on the ***Pentateuch*** (the first five books of the Bible, which is also called the *Book of the Law* or the *Torah*). They also gave special attention to the writings of the great prophets and began to collect and preserve them. They formed collections of the most popular hymns and prayers, which became the Book of Psalms. Overall, some serious collecting and editing happened.

Pentateuch—the first five books of the Bible—Genesis, Exodus, Leviticus, Numbers, and Deuteronomy

This collecting and editing continued until just before the time of Jesus. In short, what we now call the Old Testament in the Bible grew largely out of the work of the scholars and scribes of this period.

A shadow kingdom

Judah became a nation of sorts again, with its own laws and its own money, but it never regained complete independence. During this period, it lived in the shadow of Persia as a kind of subject state, and instead of restoring a monarchy, Judah became what is called a *theocracy* (a government in which it is claimed that God is the true ruler). In Judah, God was considered the king, and the high priest became God's visible representative. Therefore, the high priest had the dual role of both religious and political leader.

Check It Out

The seat of the Persian Empire was Persepolis. Persia is modern Iran.

Leaders Both Politically and Religiously

How do our Church leaders govern us both in our faith and in our politics? List two issues that are both political and religious issues.

____

____

____

____

____

____

Many of the people still clung to the promise of the coming of a messiah, a descendant of David, who would make them a great kingdom again. But until that time came, they were content to be left alone by the superpowers to worship God and to live their own lives. They made no attempts to become a military power or to expand their control over others.

Lessons learned

Many of the people finally learned to put fidelity to the covenant before all else. Both their public and their private lives became better shaped by the covenant.

They learned to appreciate the value of the religious writings that had been developing over the past thousand years. They began to recognize these writings as God's revelation to them. The reading and study of these writings, especially the messages of the prophets, became a major influence in their religious life.

Many of the people also learned to stay on guard against outside influences that had so often corrupted their faith in the past. They became suspicious, not just of other religions, but also of other cultures in general. They began to view anything non-Jewish as potentially harmful to their faith.

One key lesson underlies this experience of exile and restoration: God was still in control, still faithful to all promises made.

Think About it

What is there to be learned from this period in terms of how you regard and live your own faith?

Share your thoughts with a classmate.

Wrap-Up

After about fifty years in exile, the Jews were suddenly allowed to return home and rebuild their land. Although they had their problems, they did succeed, which included rebuilding the Temple. They experienced a complete religious reform under Ezra and they became politically organized with Nehemiah's help. Once peace was common to them, they began putting together the Bible.

What Do You Think?

Do people always have to undergo tragedies and hardships before they understand what God is asking of them? Why or why not?

What type of person doesn't need a tragedy to believe?

Reflection

The LORD is my light and my salvation;
whom shall I fear?
The LORD is the stronghold of my life;
of whom shall I be afraid?
When evildoers assail me
to devour my flesh —
my adversaries and foes —
they shall stumble and fall.
Though an army encamp against me,
my heart shall not fear;
though war rise up against me,
yet I will be confident. (Psalm 27:1–3)

Whom do you fear? Do you truly believe, like the psalmist, that God will protect and care for you if evildoers should attack you?

PRAYER FOR TODAY

Side one: Make a joyful noise to God, all the earth; sing the glory of his name; give to him glorious praise. Say to God, "How awesome are your deeds! Because of your great power, your enemies cringe before you. All the earth worships you; they sing praises to you, sing praises to your name."

Side two: Come and see what God has done: he is awesome in his deeds among mortals. He turned the sea into dry land; they passed through the river on foot. There we rejoiced in him, who rules by his might forever, whose eyes keep watch on the nations — let the rebellious not exalt themselves.

Side one: Bless our God, O peoples, let the sound of his praise be heard, who has kept us among the living, and has not let our feet slip.

Side two: For you, O God, have tested us; you have tried us as silver is tried. You brought us into the net; you laid burdens on our backs; you let people ride over our heads; we went through fire and through water; yet you have brought us out to a spacious place (Psalm 66:1–12).

All: Lord, we thank you for these Scripture lessons, which remind us that you are ever present for us, even in those most trying times. Help us remain trusting, faithful followers as we listen to the voices of the prophets in our midst. Let us ever sing your praises. Amen.

HOMEWORK

Extra Credit

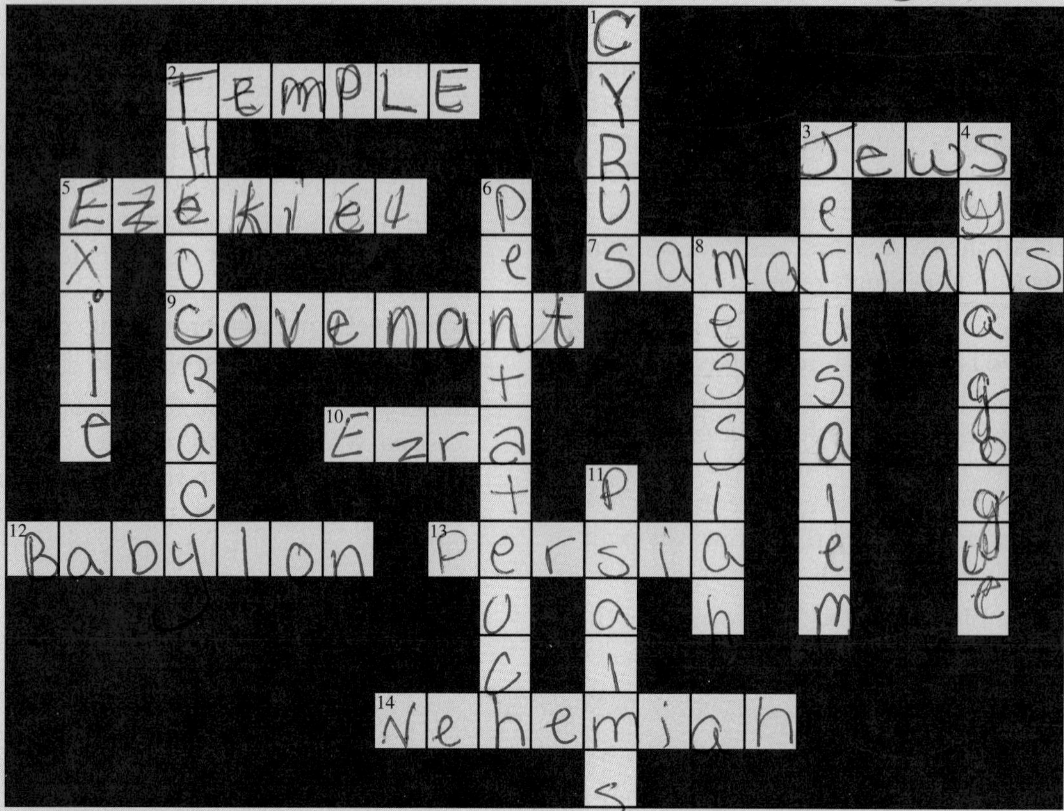

Across

2. Place of worship for Jewish people
3. People from the southern kingdom of Judah
5. Prophet who kept hope alive during the exile
7. Enemies of the Jews who tried to keep them from rebuilding their temple
9. Promise between God and God's people
10. Sometimes called the "second Moses"
12. Modern-day Iraq
13. Modern-day Iran
14. Worked with Ezra to rebuild Judea

Down

1. King of Persia who set the Jews free
2. Government in which it is claimed that God is the true ruler
3. The Holy City
4. Place of worship established while the Jews were captives in Babylon
5. A period of renewing, purifying, and deepening of faith for the chosen people
6. The first five books of the Bible
8. Descendant of David who will be sent to save God's people
11. A collection of hymns and prayers of praise

8

End of an Era

"Your house and your kingdom shall be made sure forever before me; your throne shall be established forever." (2 Samuel 7:16)

Say It with Poetry

There are many poetic writings found within the Old Testament. Read Psalm 8, and compose your own poem about your relationship with God.

Yo!

Setting the scene

The time: 333–4 B.C.E.

The place: Judea

The plot: Judah, a territory of Judea, is controlled by a series of foreign rulers during this time, beginning with Alexander the Great and ending with Rome. There are religious persecutions. There is a successful rebellion against a cruel tyrant. But through it all, Judah remains faithful to God and its expectation of the messiah grows among some groups of Jews.

Who's who?

Alexander the Great—coming out of Greece, Alexander conquered Persia and ruled from Greece to India. Judah became a tiny part of his empire.

Antiochus IV—a cruel tyrant who tried to force Judah to worship Greek gods; defiled the Temple

Maccabeus brothers: Judas, Jonathan, and Simon—lead the people in a successful rebellion against Antiochus IV

Pharisees, Sadducees, Essenes—three Jewish religious sects that promoted their own versions of religious reform

Freedom Under Another's Rule

Make a list of five freedoms that you have in your household.

1. ______________________________
2. ______________________________
3. ______________________________
4. ______________________________
5. ______________________________

Now, make a list of five rules that you have in your household.

1. ______________________________
2. ______________________________
3. ______________________________
4. ______________________________
5. ______________________________

Discuss with the class what it is like to have freedom in a household that is run by your parents and their rules.

Freedom Isn't Always Free

Have you ever had a freedom taken away because you broke someone else's rules? What was the freedom? What did you miss most about not having the freedom? Did you appreciate your freedom more when it was returned to you?

Conquerors come and go

Alexander seemed to come out of nowhere, taking over for his father Philip in 336 B.C.E. In just thirteen years, he established the largest empire yet known to history. When Alexander defeated the old Persian empire in 331 B.C.E., Judah came under his control. With no more worlds to conquer, Alexander died suddenly in 323 B.C.E. at the age of thirty-three.

From around 300 B.C.E. to 200 B.C.E., the Ptolemies of Egypt controlled Judah, but they left the Jews alone to worship as they wished. This changed in 198 B.C.E., when the Seleucids of Syria defeated Egypt and took control of Judah. Unlike Egypt, Syria had completely adopted the Greek culture and its gods. So when Syria began to rule Judah, it tried to force the Greek culture and religion on the people.

The real villain of this period was the Syrian king, Antiochus IV, who liked to call himself *Epiphanes*. Antiochus considered himself the epiphany of the Greek god Zeus. In 167 B.C.E., he passed laws demanding that the Jews worship him and the other Greek gods. Those who refused risked torture and death. Antiochus even turned the Temple into a Greek temple filled with statues of Greek gods.

Epiphany—Greek word meaning "to display or show"

Super Powers—small-group activity

In your opinion, which countries have the greatest influence on other countries?

In a small group, compare your responses and come to a consensus on the top three most powerful countries in the world.

1.

2.

3.

Maccabean rebellion

To the credit of the people, many chose martyrdom rather than be unfaithful to the God of Abraham. One of the most famous stories of this kind of courage is found in 2 Maccabees. Seven brothers, encouraged by their mother, endured terrible torture and death rather than give up faith in their God. It was about this time that the Book of Daniel appeared, recalling the bravery of the Jews who refused to obey similar laws during their captivity in Babylon. It was this book that gave courage to the Jews during these persecutions.

Scripture Search

Read 2 Maccabees, chapter 7.

1. Would it have been harder or easier to be one of the last brothers to be tortured? Why?

2. Have you ever risked standing out from the crowd to perform a Christian act or behavior? Have you ever encouraged another person to perform a Christian action that took great courage on their part? Describe this experience.

In 166 B.C.E., the people rallied to rebellion. This rebellion started as guerrilla warfare, where they hid in the hills, launched surprise attacks, and then returned to hide. By 164 B.C.E., they succeeded in recapturing and purifying the Temple. In 142 B.C.E., Judah actually won its independence from Syria.

Check It Out

The Jewish Feast of Lights or Hanukkah, a popular and joyous Jewish feast, recalls the time Judas Maccabeus recaptured the Temple after defeating Antiochus in 164 B.C.E.

The Winner

Imagine that your team is the winner in a regional baseball tournament. To claim the state title, you now have to play the winner of the Major League World Series. How do you feel about winning your regional tournament? What do you think are your chances of winning the state tournament? Discuss with your class how this scenario is similar to Judah's.

Rome, the new superpower

Actually, to say Judah became independent is misleading. It's true that Judah did enjoy a degree of religious freedom, but it was a tiny nation living in the shadow of giants. Despite its success at guerrilla warfare, it had no real army to speak of. Judah was fair game as it remained at the mercy of any larger nations that decided to conquer it.

By 100 B.C.E., Rome began to flex its muscles in this region. Egypt, Syria, and Greece were tired old empires and proved to be no match for Rome's power. By 63 B.C.E., the Roman general Pompey entered Jerusalem with his army. It was inevitable for Judah to come under Roman control, where it eventually stayed for several centuries. Rome's powerful army continued on to conquer the entire Middle East.

To Judah's advantage, Rome had a policy of allowing its conquered lands to govern themselves, provided they stay loyal to Rome. So the chosen people were allowed to follow their own religion, as long as it didn't foster rebellion against Rome. Rome even set up a kind of Jewish kingdom and gave it a puppet king, Herod the Great. This is the political situation when the Old Testament ends.

Check It Out

Although the Romans conquered the Greeks with their armies, the Greeks conquered the Romans with their ideas.

In the last century before Jesus, three different Jewish religious sects developed, each with its own idea of what it meant to be faithful to the covenant.

Essenes

The Essenes were a kind of religious community that lived apart from the people and tried to avoid all contact with the foreign culture. They held all property in common and followed the Law of Moses to the last detail. They prayed, fasted, and studied the prophets. They expected the coming of the Messiah and the end of the world. (Some scholars think John the Baptizer might have spent some time among the Essenes.)

Pharisees

The Pharisees taught strict following of the Law of Moses and applied it to every detail of daily life. They did not try to live apart from others as the Essenes did. Instead, they tried to make civil law and religious law the same. All law was seen as a protection of the covenant and a guarantee of faithful observance.

Sadducees

Many members of the Saducees were priests. They tended to like much of the Greek and Roman culture and saw no harm in it. They also felt it was usually better to compromise with the ruling powers of the day and even to bend the religious rules if it meant keeping peace. They interpreted the Law of Moses much more loosely. Needless to say, the Pharisees and Sadducees didn't always agree.

Check It Out

When Pompey conquered Jerusalem, he went into the Temple looking for the Jewish god. He laughed after he entered the Holy of Holies and didn't find a single statue.

Heaven

Use the letters in the word *heaven* to describe what you believe heaven will be like and where heaven may be.

H ______________________________

E ______________________________

A ______________________________

V ______________________________

E ______________________________

N ______________________________

Life after death

A major new insight into faith developed among some groups of Jews during this last century before Jesus. It was the idea of personal immortality and the resurrection of the dead. Though there were traces of these beliefs throughout the Old Testament, especially in the books of the prophets and the Psalms, they were not well developed or widely held among the people. During the time of the Maccabees, as people faced persecution and martyrdom, the conviction grew that God would reward them for their fidelity; therefore, opening the door for the belief of rewards after death in a life everlasting.

Scripture Search

Read 2 Maccabees 7:20–23.

If we knew for sure that there would be no life after this one, how would the world be different? How would people act?

____

____

____

____

____

How strong is your own belief in an eternal life after this one? How does it affect your life decisions?

____

____

____

____

____

Messiah as the Hero

Describe a situation where you might need a hero. What five qualities would you want your hero to have? Do these qualities fit the person of Jesus? If so, could Jesus be the "hero" that we are looking for?

____

____

____

____

____

____

Messianism

It was also during this period that hope in the coming of the messiah became very popular among some Jewish groups. Many began to talk about the day when the messiah would come and restore Israel to its greatness. If you recall, the promise of a messiah has its roots in the promise God made to David in 2 Samuel 7:16, when God said that David's throne would last forever.

Messiah—Hebrew word meaning "anointed one." The word *Christ* has the same meaning in Greek.

The prophets, especially Isaiah, began to share their ideas about what kind of person this messiah would be. They believed the person would be a great and just king, an heir of David, who would come and restore David's kingdom to glory. This idea was kept alive and further developed by other prophets, such as Micah, Ezekiel, and Daniel.

Messiah = ? small-group activity

In small groups, rewrite the nativity story in today's terms. If Jesus were to come to earth today, where might he be born? Who might his parents be? Who would be there to greet him? Share your story with the other groups.

By the time of Jesus, David's throne had been under the rule of foreign powers continually for almost 600 years. People were tired of it and impatient for a return to having their own king. There had been an absence of prophets in the land for almost 300 years. John the Baptizer suddenly appeared in the desert looking like a prophet of old and proclaiming that the messiah was at hand. He had no trouble drawing a crowd of believers for they were eager for his message.

Specifically, some people were looking for a "political" messiah, an earthly ruler who could rally the people, lead an army, drive out the hated invaders, and avenge all the past injustices. These people certainly weren't looking for a messiah who would come out of Nazareth preaching "Blessed are the poor, the meek, the merciful, the persecuted." But that's what they got. So ends our story of the Old Testament, which opens the door for the story of the New Testament to begin!

Scripture Search

Read the following passages to discover the kind of "savior" some people were expecting their messiah to be. Read the passages from Isaiah and Luke to discover whom they got.

2 Samuel 22:2–4

Isaiah 19:20

Jeremiah 14:8–9

Isaiah 11:1–9 and Luke 2:10–11

Check It Out

Herod the Great, the Jewish king who ruled at the time of Jesus' birth, greatly expanded the Temple that was rebuilt in Ezra and Nehemiah's day. He added porticos and porches, among other things. It was this expanded temple that Jesus knew.

Lessons learned

You've been following the history of the children of Abraham over a period of almost two thousand years. During that time, God patiently and carefully taught the people certain truths. Here's a summary of the key lessons of the Old Testament.

The God of Abraham is the only, the all-powerful God, Creator and Ruler of all things. He is merciful, patient, gentle, loving, and concerned for each individual.

Above all, God is faithful. When God made a special covenant with Abraham, and then with Abraham's children, he promised to remain faithful always!

The Passover–Exodus–covenant and the conquest of the promised land are the core events of the Israelites' history. These experiences developed the foundations of Israel's faith in God.

In hindsight, all other major events in Israel's history took on new meaning in light of these core events.

Even when situations seemed totally hopeless, God again and again rescued the chosen people. Therefore, fidelity to God means, first of all, always trusting in their God rather than worshiping the "false gods" of wealth, earthly power, and influence. Second, fidelity to the covenant means treating others justly, especially those unable to protect and care for themselves.

Whenever the Israelites became unfaithful to God, relied on false gods, or treated one another unjustly, they brought defeat and suffering upon themselves.

God was always ready to forgive and restore them when they repented.

God spoke through the prophets, people especially called and sent by God to speak to Israel in his name. The prophets called the people back to fidelity when they strayed from the covenant. The prophets also helped the people deepen their understanding of God and his plan for creation.

Central to that plan was the promise to send a messiah who would establish God's kingdom of peace, unity, and justice among all people, and who would lead all people to worship God.

God is not impressed or fooled by external, empty religious rituals and sacrifices that are not backed up by sincerity of heart and just actions that are in keeping with the covenant.

Obviously, this list is just a thumbnail sketch of the main truths revealed in the Old Testament.

Nuggets of Treasure

Remember the treasure hunt in the introduction of this book? Turn to it now. How many answers have you unearthed since you began this treasure hunt through the Old Testament?

____

____

____

____

____

____

What Do You Think?

Do you think you are now able to understand better what you read in the Old Testament? Why or why not?

____

____

____

____

____

____

____

____

Wrap-Up

Well, there you have it. The next time you hear a reading from the Old Testament at Mass, hopefully it will have a familiar ring to it. You'll be able to recognize some names, recall some stories, and possibly remember the events surrounding the reading. You now have the power to have an even better personal respect for the ancient writings than Indiana Jones did in the classic *Raiders of the Lost Ark*. Take this power seriously and you will find great success in your faith life.

A final note

You really can't understand the New Testament or Christian Scriptures (part two of the story) without knowing the Hebrew Scriptures and the other books of the Old Testament. In the same way, once you know "the rest of the story," which the New Testament gives you, you get new insights into the first part of the story. The teachings of the prophets, for example, take on new meaning when you read them in light of the teachings and actions of Jesus. It's somewhat like reading a mystery novel. Once you get to the end and discover "who did it," then you begin to recall and recognize all the clues that didn't seem important when you first read them.

Reflection

Remember your creator in the days of your youth, before the days of trouble come, and the years draw near when you will say, "I have no pleasure in them" . . . and the dust returns to the earth as it was, and the breath returns to God who gave it. Vanity of vanities, says the Teacher; all is vanity. (Ecclesiastes 12:1, 7–8)

How are you spending the youth God has entrusted to you?

Are you too concerned with "vanities"?

Do you give enough attention to your relationship with God?

PRAYER FOR TODAY

Leader: As we complete our study of the Hebrew Scriptures, let us remember that the lessons taught to the chosen people are lessons for us also. Listen to the following reading, and discover that we are the people mentioned in these verses.

Reader: For you are a people holy to the LORD your God; the LORD your God has chosen you out of all the peoples on earth to be his people, his treasured possession. It was not because you were more numerous than any other people that the LORD set his heart on you and chose you—for you were the fewest of all peoples. It was because the LORD loved you and kept the oath that he swore to your ancestors, that the LORD has brought you out with a mighty hand, and redeemed you from the house of slavery, from the hand of Pharaoh king of Egypt. Know therefore that the LORD your God is God, the faithful God who maintains covenant loyalty with those who love him and keep his commandments, to a thousand generations (Deuteronomy 7:6–9).

Side one: Lord, we praise you for your faithfulness, in spite of our lack of trust in your love and concern for us. Let us never forget the lessons of our ancestors in faith. Help us remember that this world and everything in it belongs to God.

Side two: Let us live mindful of the presence of God's glory and majesty all around us. Let us celebrate God's love for us by living our lives for others and dedicating our works to the service of the Lord.

All: Amen. Alleluia.

COURSE EVALUATION

Answer the following questions.

1. What did you most like about this course?

2. What is the most important thing you think you learned in this course?

3. What was the most surprising thing you learned about your faith during this course?

4. From the summary of faith lessons on page 90 in chapter 8, list the three faith lessons that you feel are the most important for you at this point in your life.

Appendix I

GOD'S PRESENCE AS SEEN THROUGHOUT SCRIPTURE

God's Presence in Creation

Genesis 1:1–2:3

1 In the beginning when God created the
heavens and the earth, 2 the earth was a
formless void and darkness covered the
face of the deep, while a wind from God
swept over the face of the waters. 3 Then
God said, "Let there be light"; and there
was light. 4 And God saw that the light
was good; and God separated the light
from the darkness. 5 God called the light
Day, and the darkness he called Night.
And there was evening and there was
morning, the first day.

6 And God said, "Let there be a dome in
the midst of the waters, and let it separate
the waters from the waters." 7 So God
made the dome and separated the waters
that were under the dome from the waters
that were above the dome. And it was so.
8 God called the dome Sky. And there was
evening and there was morning, the
second day.

9 And God said, "Let the waters under the
sky be gathered together into one place,
and let the dry land appear." And it was so.
10 God called the dry land Earth, and the
waters that were gathered together he
called Seas. And God saw that it was
good. 11 Then God said, "Let the earth put
forth vegetation: plants yielding seed, and
fruit trees of every kind on earth that bear
fruit with the seed in it." And it was so.
12 The earth brought forth vegetation:
plants yielding seed of every kind, and
trees of every kind bearing fruit with the
seed in it. And God saw that it was good.
13 And there was evening and there was
morning, the third day.

14 And God said, "Let there be lights in
the dome of the sky to separate the day
from the night; and let them be for signs
and for seasons and for days and years,
15 and let them be lights in the dome of the
sky to give light upon the earth." And it
was so. 16 God made the two great lights—
the greater light to rule the day and the
lesser light to rule the night—and the stars.
17 God set them in the dome of the sky to
give light upon the earth, 18 to rule over the
day and over the night, and to separate the
light from the darkness. And God saw that
it was good. 19 And there was evening and
there was morning, the fourth day.

20 And God said, "Let the waters bring
forth swarms of living creatures, and let
birds fly above the earth across the dome
of the sky." 21 So God created the great sea
monsters and every living creature that
moves, of every kind, with which the
waters swarm, and every winged bird of
every kind. And God saw that it was good.
22 God blessed them, saying, "Be fruitful

and multiply and fill the waters in the
seas, and let birds multiply on the earth."
[23] And there was evening and there was
morning, the fifth day.
[24] And God said, "Let the earth bring
forth living creatures of every kind: cattle
and creeping things and wild animals of
the earth of every kind." And it was so.
[25] God made the wild animals of the earth
of every kind, and the cattle of every kind,
and everything that creeps upon the
ground of every kind. And God saw that
it was good.
[26] Then God said, "Let us make human-
kind in our image, according to our likeness;
and let them have dominion over the fish of
the sea, and over the birds of the air, and
over the cattle, and over all the wild animals
of the earth, and over every creeping thing
that creeps upon the earth."

[27] So God created humankind in his image,
in the image of God he created them; male
and female he created them.
[28] God blessed them, and God said to
them, "Be fruitful and multiply, and fill the
earth and subdue it; and have dominion
over the fish of the sea and over the birds
of the air and over every living thing that
moves upon the earth." [29] God said, "See, I
have given you every plant yielding seed
that is upon the face of all the earth, and
every tree with seed in its fruit; you shall
have them for food. [30] And to every beast
of the earth, and to every bird of the air,
and to everything that creeps on the earth,
everything that has the breath of life, I
have given every green plant for food."
And it was so. [31] God saw everything that
he had made, and indeed, it was very
good. And there was evening and there
was morning, the sixth day.

God's Presence in the Rainbow

Genesis 9:8–16

[8] Then God said to Noah and to his sons
with him, [9] "As for me, I am establishing
my covenant with you and your descen-
dants after you, [10] and with every living
creature that is with you, the birds, the
domestic animals, and every animal of
the earth with you, as many as came out
of the ark. [11] I establish my covenant with
you, that never again shall all flesh be cut
off by the waters of a flood, and never
again shall there be a flood to destroy the
earth." [12] God said, "This is the sign of the
covenant that I make between me and
you and every living creature that is with
you, for all future generations: [13] I have
set my bow in the clouds, and it shall be a
sign of the covenant between me and the
earth. [14] When I bring clouds over the
earth and the bow is seen in the clouds,
[15] I will remember my covenant that is
between me and you and every living
creature of all flesh; and the waters shall
never again become a flood to destroy all
flesh. [16] When the bow is in the clouds, I
will see it and remember the everlasting
covenant between God and every living
creature of all flesh that is on the earth."

God's Presence in the Burning Bush

Exodus 3:1–6

1 Moses was keeping the flock of his
father-in-law Jethro, the priest of Midian;
he led his flock beyond the wilderness,
and came to Horeb, the mountain of God.
2 There the angel of the LORD appeared to
him in a flame of fire out of a bush; he
looked, and the bush was blazing, yet it
was not consumed. 3 Then Moses said, "I
must turn aside and look at this great
sight, and see why the bush is not burned
up." 4 When the LORD saw that he had
turned aside to see, God called to him out
of the bush, "Moses, Moses!" And he said,
"Here I am." 5 Then he said, "Come no
closer! Remove the sandals from your feet,
for the place on which you are standing is
holy ground." 6 He said further, "I am the
God of your father, the God of Abraham,
the God of Isaac, and the God of Jacob."
And Moses hid his face, for he was afraid
to look at God.

God's Presence in the Manna in the Desert

Exodus 16:14–15

[14] When the layer of dew lifted, there on the surface of the wilderness was a fine flaky substance, as fine as frost on the ground. [15] When the Israelites saw it, they said to one another, "What is it?" For they did not know what it was. Moses said to them, "It is the bread that the LORD has given you to eat.

[31] The house of Israel called it manna; it was like coriander seed, white, and the taste of it was like wafers made with honey. [32] Moses said, "This is what the LORD has commanded: 'Let an omer of it be kept throughout your generations, in order that they may see the food with which I fed you in the wilderness, when I brought you out of the land of Egypt.' "

God's Presence in the Pillar of Cloud and Pillar of Fire

Exodus 13:21–22

[21] The LORD went in front of them in a pillar of cloud by day, to lead them along the way, and in a pillar of fire by night, to give them light, so that they might travel by day and by night. [22] Neither the pillar of cloud by day nor the pillar of fire by night left its place in front of the people.

God's Presence through the Ten Commandments

Deuteronomy 5:1–22

1 Moses convened all Israel, and said to them:

Hear, O Israel, the statutes and ordinances that I am addressing to you today; you shall learn them and observe them diligently. 2 The LORD our God made a covenant with us at Horeb. 3 Not with our ancestors did the LORD make this covenant, but with us, who are all of us here alive today. 4 The LORD spoke with you face to face at the mountain, out of the fire. 5 (At that time I was standing between the LORD and you to declare to you the words of the LORD; for you were afraid because of the fire and did not go up the mountain.) And he said:

6 I am the LORD your God, who brought you out of the land of Egypt, out of the house of slavery; 7 you shall have no other gods before me.

8 You shall not make for yourself an idol, whether in the form of anything that is in heaven above, or that is on the earth beneath, or that is in the water under the earth. 9 You shall not bow down to them or worship them; for I the LORD your God am a jealous God, punishing children for the iniquity of parents, to the third and fourth generation of those who reject me, 10 but showing steadfast love to the thousandth generation of those who love me and keep my commandments.

11 You shall not make wrongful use of the name of the LORD your God, for the LORD will not acquit anyone who misuses his name.

12 Observe the sabbath day and keep it holy, as the LORD your God commanded you. 13 Six days you shall labor and do all your work. 14 But the seventh day is a sabbath to the LORD your God; you shall not do any work — you, or your son or your daughter, or your male or female slave, or your ox or your donkey, or any of your livestock, or the resident alien in your towns, so that your male and female slave may rest as well as you. 15 Remember that you were a slave in the land of Egypt, and the LORD your God brought you out from there with a mighty hand and an outstretched arm; therefore the LORD your God commanded you to keep the sabbath day.

16 Honor your father and your mother, as the LORD your God commanded you, so that your days may be long and that it may go well with you in the land that the LORD your God is giving you.

17 You shall not murder.

18 Neither shall you commit adultery.

19 Neither shall you steal.

20 Neither shall you bear false witness against your neighbor.

21 Neither shall you covet your neighbor's wife.

Neither shall you desire your neighbor's house, or field, or male or female slave, or ox, or donkey, or anything that belongs to your neighbor.

22 These words the LORD spoke with a loud voice to your whole assembly at the mountain, out of the fire, the cloud, and the thick darkness, and he added no more. He wrote them on two stone tablets, and gave them to me.

God's Presence in the Silence

1 Kings 19:9–13

9 Then the word of the LORD came to
him, saying, "What are you doing here,
Elijah?" 10 He answered, "I have been very
zealous for the LORD, the God of hosts; for
the Israelites have forsaken your covenant,
thrown down your altars, and killed your
prophets with the sword. I alone am left,
and they are seeking my life, to take it
away."

11 He said, "Go out and stand on the
mountain before the LORD, for the LORD
is about to pass by." Now there was a
great wind, so strong that it was splitting
mountains and breaking rocks in pieces
before the LORD, but the LORD was
not in the wind; and after the wind an
earthquake, but the LORD was not in the
earthquake; 12 and after the earthquake a
fire, but the LORD was not in the fire;
and after the fire a sound of sheer
silence. 13 When Elijah heard it, he
wrapped his face in his mantle and went
out and stood at the entrance of the cave.
Then there came a voice to him that said,
"What are you doing here, Elijah?"

God's Presence in the Promise of a New Covenant

2 Samuel 7:8–12

8 Now therefore thus you shall say to
my servant David: Thus says the LORD of
hosts: I took you from the pasture, from
following the sheep to be prince over my
people Israel; 9 and I have been with you
wherever you went, and have cut off all
your enemies from before you; and I will
make for you a great name, like the name
of the great ones of the earth. 10 And I will
appoint a place for my people Israel and
will plant them, so that they may live in
their own place, and be disturbed no
more; and evildoers shall afflict them no
more, as formerly, 11 from the time that I
appointed judges over my people Israel;
and I will give you rest from all your
enemies. Moreover the LORD declares to
you that the LORD will make you a house.
12 When your days are fulfilled and you lie
down with your ancestors, I will raise up
your offspring after you, who shall come
forth from your body, and I will establish
his kingdom.

God's Presence in the Keeping of a Promise

Luke 1:26–27

26 In the sixth month the angel Gabriel
was sent by God to a town in Galilee
called Nazareth, 27 to a virgin engaged to a
man whose name was Joseph, of the house
of David. The virgin's name was Mary.

God's Presence in the Word Made Flesh

Luke 2:1–16

1 In those days a decree went out from Emperor Augustus that all the world should be registered. 2 This was the first registration and was taken while Quirinius was governor of Syria. 3 All went to their own towns to be registered. 4 Joseph also went from the town of Nazareth in Galilee to Judea, to the city of David called Bethlehem, because he was descended from the house and family of David. 5 He went to be registered with Mary, to whom he was engaged and who was expecting a child. 6 While they were there, the time came for her to deliver her child. 7 And she gave birth to her firstborn son and wrapped him in bands of cloth, and laid him in a manger, because there was no place for them in the inn.

8 In that region there were shepherds living in the fields, keeping watch over their flock by night. 9 Then an angel of the Lord stood before them, and the glory of the Lord shone around them, and they were terrified. 10 But the angel said to them, "Do not be afraid; for see — I am bringing you good news of great joy for all the people: 11 to you is born this day in the city of David a Savior, who is the Messiah, the Lord. 12 This will be a sign for you: you will find a child wrapped in bands of cloth and lying in a manger." 13 And suddenly there was with the angel a multitude of the heavenly host, praising God and saying,

14 "Glory to God in the highest heaven, and on earth peace among those whom he favors!"

15 When the angels had left them and gone into heaven, the shepherds said to one another, "Let us go now to Bethlehem and see this thing that has taken place, which the Lord has made known to us." 16 So they went with haste and found Mary and Joseph, and the child lying in the manger.

". . . this day in the city of David . . ."

Appendix II

YOUR CATHOLIC HERITAGE

Traditional Prayers

Sign of the Cross

In the name of the Father,
and of the Son,
and of the Holy Spirit.
Amen.

The Lord's Prayer

Our Father, who art in heaven,
hallowed be your name;
Your kingdom come;
Your will be done on earth
as it is in heaven.
Give us this day our daily bread;
and forgive us our trespasses
as we forgive those
who trespass against us;
and lead us not into temptation,
but deliver us from evil. Amen.

Hail Mary

Hail, Mary, full of grace, the Lord is with you!
Blessed are you among women, and blessed
is the fruit of your womb, Jesus.
Holy Mary, Mother of God, pray for us
sinners, now and at the hour of our death.
Amen.

Trinity Prayer

Glory to the Father,
and to the Son,
and to the Holy Spirit.
As it was in the beginning, is now,
and will be forever. Amen.

Señal de la Cruz

En el nombre del Padre
y del Hijo
y del Espíritu Santo.
Amén.

Padre Nuestro

Padre nuestro, que estás en el cielo,
santificado sea to nombre;
venga tu reino;
hágase tu voluntad en el tierrs
como en el cielo.
Danos hay nuestro pan de cade día;
perdona nuestras ofensas como también
nosotros perdonamos a los que nos ofenden;
no nos dejes caer en tentación,
y líbranos del mal. Amén.

Ave Maria

Dios te salve, María, llena eres de gracia,
el Señor es contigo,
bendita Tú eres entre todas las mujeres,
y bendito es el fruto de tu vientre, Jesús.
Santa María, Madre de Dios,
ruéga por nosotros pecadores,
ahora y en la hora de nuestra muerte.
Amén.

Gloria

Gloria al Padre y al Hijo y al Espíritu Santo.
Como era en el principio ahora y siempre
por los siglos de los siglos. Amén.

Rules Catholics Live By

The Law of Love

"Love one another as I have loved you."
(John 15:12)

The Ten Commandments

1. I, the Lord, am your God. You shall not have other gods besides me.
2. You shall not take the name of the Lord, your God, in vain.
3. Remember to keep holy the Sabbath day.
4. Honor your father and your mother.
5. You shall not kill.
6. You shall not commit adultery.
7. You shall not steal.
8. You shall not bear false witness against your neighbor.
9. You shall not covet your neighbor's wife.
10. You shall not covet anything that belongs to your neighbor.

The Great Commandments

"Love the Lord your God
with all your heart,
with all your soul,
with all your strength, and
with all your mind;
love your neighbor as you love yourself."
(Luke 10:27; see Deuteronomy 6:5; Leviticus 19:18)

Laws of the Church

1. Keep Sundays holy and participate in Mass on Sunday and holy days of obligation.
2. Lead a sacramental life, frequently receiving the Eucharist.
3. Prepare for Confirmation and be confirmed.
4. Observe the marriage laws of the Church and provide whildren with religious training.
5. Strengthen and support the Church.
6. Do penance, including abstaining from meat and fasting from food on appointed days.
7. Join in the missionary spirit and works of the Church.

Works of Mercy

Corporal Works of Mercy

1. Feed the hungry.
2. Give drink to the thirsty.
3. Clothe the naked.
4. Shelter the homeless.
5. Visit the sick.
6. Visit the imprisoned.
7. Bury the dead.

Spiritual Works of Mercy

1. Counsel the doubtful.
2. Instruct the ignorant.
3. Admonish the sinner.
4. Comfort the sorrowful.
5. Forgive injuries.
6. Bear wrongs patiently.
7. Pray for the living and the dead.

What Catholics Believe

Nicene Creed

We believe in one God,
the Father, the Almighty,
maker of heaven and earth,
of all that is seen and unseen.
We believe in one Lord, Jesus Christ,
the only Son of God,
eternally begotten of the Father,
God from God, Light from Light,
true God from true God,
begotten, not made, one in being with the Father.
Through him all things were made.
For us men and our slavation
he came down from heaven:
by the power of the Holy Spirit
he was born of the Virgin Mary, and became man.
For our sake he was crucified under Pontius Pilate;
he suffered, died, and was buried.
On the third day he rose again
in fulfillment of the Scriptures;
he ascended into heaven
and is seated at the right hand of the Father.
He will come again in glory to judge the living and the dead,
and his kingdom will have no end.
We believein the Holy Spirit, the Lord, the giver of life,
who proceeds from the Father and the Son.
With the Father and the Son he is worshiped and glorified.
He has spoken through the Prophets.
We believe in one, holy, catholic, and apostolic Church.
We acknowledge one baptism for the forgiveness of sins.
We look for the resurrection of the dead,

Eucharistic Prayer IV

Father, we acknowledge your greatness:
all your actions show your wisdom and love.
You formed man in your own likeness
and set him over the whole world
to serve you, his creator,
and to rule over all creatures.
Even when he disobeyed you and lost your friendship,
you did not abandon him to the power of death,
but helped all men to seek and find you.
Again and again you offered a covenant to man,
and through the prophets taught him to hope for salvation.
Father, you so loved the world
that in the fullness of time you sent
your only Son to be our Savior.
He was conceived through the power
of the Holy Spirit, and born of the Virgin Mary,
a man like us in all things but sin.
To the poor he proclaimed
the good news of salvation, to prisoners, freedom,
and to those in sorrow, joy.
In fulfillment of your will
he gave himself up to death;
but by rising from the dead,
he destroyed death and restored life.
And that we might live no longer for
ourselves but for him,
he sent the Holy Spirit from you, Father,
as his first gift to those who believe,
to complete his work on earth
and bring us the fullness of grace.
Father, may this Holy Spirit
sanctify these offerings.
Let them become the body
and blood of Jesus Christ our Lord
as we celebrate the great mystery
which he left us as an everlasting covenant. . . .

Catholic Devotions and Practices

The Rosary

The Joyful Mysteries

(Mondays and Thursdays)

1. The annunciation
2. The visitation
3. The birth of Jesus
4. The presentation in the temple
5. Mary and Joseph find Jesus in the Temple

The Sorrowful Mysteries

(Tuesdays and Fridays)

1. The agony in the garden
2. The scourging of Jesus
3. The crowning with thorns
4. Jesus carries his cross
5. Jesus dies on the cross

The Glorious Mysteries

(Sundays, Wednesdays, and Saturdays)

1. The resurrection
2. The ascension
3. The Holy Spirit is sent upon the apostles
4. The assumption of Mary
5. Mary is crowned queen of heaven and earth

Holy Days

Christmas, the birth of Jesus—December 25

Solemnity of Mary, Mother of God—January 1

Ascension of the Lord—the fortieth day (Thursday) after Easter

Assumption of Mary into heaven—August 15

All Saints' Day—November 1

Immaculate Conception of Mary—December 8

Stations of the Cross

First Station: Jesus is condemned to death.

Second Station: Jesus is made to carry his cross.

Third Station: Jesus falls for the first time.

Fourth Station: Jesus meets Mary, his mother.

Fifth Station: Simon, the Cyrenian, helps Jesus carry his cross.

Sixth Station: Veronica wipes the face of Jesus.

Seventh Station: Jesus falls the second time.

Eighth Station: Jesus speaks to the daughter of Jerusalem.

Ninth Station: Jesus falls the third time.

Tenth Station: Jesus is stripped of his garments.

Eleventh Station: Jesus is nailed to the cross.

Twelfth Station: Jesus dies on the cross.

Thirteenth Station: Jesus is taken down from the cross.

Fourteenth Station: Jesus is laid in the tomb.

Days of Fasting

(Days when Catholics eighteen to fifty-nine eat only one full meal)

Ash Wednesday

Good Friday

Days of Abstinence

(Days when Catholics age fourteen and over do not eat meat)

Ash Wednesday

Fridays in Lent

Good Friday